CW01521479

A Little Book Of Lies

or

Penguin Gynaecology for Beginners

3RD and Final Edition

**AN ANALOGUE WARMTH
PUBLICATION**

A Little Book of Lies
or
Penguin Gynaecology for Beginners (3rd Edition.)
by
Richard Lockwood & Steven Potz-Rayner
with illustrations by
Angela Creasey

This edition published 2013 by
Analogue Warmth

The authors assert the moral right under the Copyright,
Designs and Patents Act 1988 to be identified as the authors
of this work.

All Rights reserved. No part of this publication may be
reproduced, stored in a retrieval system, or transmitted, in
any form or by any means without the prior written consent
of the author, nor be otherwise circulated in any form of
binding or cover other than that in which it is published and
without a similar condition being imposed on the subsequent
purchaser.

Copyright © Richard Lockwood & Steven Potz-Rayner
2006, 2008, 2013

Photography of Mr Lockwood by Tim Morgan

The photograph of Mr Potz-Rayner is a chin disguising 'selfie'
as the young folk say.

With thanks to Chris Muskett, Tim Morgan and
Joanna Potz-Rayner for their contributions

Original Introduction to the First Edition

by Dr J. Gammon

Welcome to the Little Book Of Lies (alternatively titled Penguin Gynaecology for Beginners), a tome that has already been universally agreed by acknowledged leaders in the field as the most significant, forthright and intellectually devastating collection of lies and misleading statements ever to have been collected together in one place; and if not definitively 'ever' then at least since the Labour Party Manifesto of 1997.

It is a sad reflection that in recent years, society has begun to frown on the telling of lies and deceits, instead favouring the far more prosaic and frankly woolly concept of 'truth'. Indeed, several serial liars have even spent time at Her Majesty's Pleasure merely for forging the truth, completely at odds with the actuality of the machinations of Government and the treatment of liars throughout history in general – at odds with the fact that the thinking behind some of history's great philosophical tracts has been sparked off by some completely spurious facts regarding racing pigeons, jam and the inside leg measurement of King Edward II.

This book seeks to rectify that situation in some small way by providing you, the reader, with a collection of lies of the highest quality, all of which have been individually tested to near expiry in the Royal Courts of Siam, The People's Republic of Moldavia, the European Court Of Truth Distortion In The Interest Of Arms Deals And Other Shady Activity and the CIA not to mention senior academics across the breadth of the UK, many of whom cannot be named here for their own personal safety. It goes without saying that while you cradle a shade over eighteen hundred lies in this edition, more than ninety thousand were rejected at any of the forty-six quality control stages this book has passed through at the hands of these various fine establishments, people and states of mind.

Your utilisation of this book of lies is entirely up to you. You may wish to keep it in the smallest room of the house, to dip into in those moments of quiet contemplation, or you might enjoy using it as a source of 'knowledge' with which to amaze and astound your friends, relations and colleagues. Assuming they're worrying gullible that is.

One should at all times bear in mind that none of what follows in this book is true. Not a single thing bears even the slightest resemblance to actual fact, and if anything should then it is purely be co-incidence and was at no time intended, implied or otherwise construed. It is not the intention of the authors to imply any wrong-doing, deviant behaviour or criminal activity by well-known figures of stage, screen, athletic track or late night 'sauna' who may be mentioned in the forthcoming pages, nor is it their intention to actually mislead the reader - rather, they merely hope to raise a smile and a chuckle. As such all lawyers are asked to note that any hope of legal recrimination is on a hiding to nothing and they should put down the sports car magazines now.

Be warned though, that after reading these lies your level of trust in the printed word may diminish in much the same way that after watching a television show of outtakes from assorted allegedly loved televisual feasts you fully expect the set of your favourite soap opera to collapse. Essentially, your expectations will become remodelled in much the same way that Kuala Lumpur was once a small town on Madagascar before a time vortex sucked it up and spat it out several hundred miles away with a totally different structure and populace.

Alas, it will never happen and you'll not see Albert Square reduced to a pile of radioactive rubble, no matter how hard you wish, nor to which deities you present sacrificial offerings. Not even if the authors and I join you in your prayers. Alas, that is no lie. Sorry.

Dr. J. Gammon BSE, BSC, MSC, CPT, FRCS, HTFC, ELO

University of Cleckheaton.

Introduction to the Second Edition

By The Very Revd. Kenneth Sputum

Hello. I'm Ken Sputum, noted archaeologist, cheese frotter and kidney bruiser. Yes ladies, you know what I'm talking about, form a queue. Welcome to the Second Edition of the Little Book of Lies.

Since it was originally published in 1422 the apathy has been overwhelming. More than 150 copies of the original volume were sold, or bought anyway. Rumour has it that many were given away free with thirty quids worth of diesel after an unfortunate garage owner with a penchant of penguin porn and gin and in possession of a credit card one alcohol-fuelled internet-connected night bought a box load thinking he was on for some no holds barred non-flying feathery filth. Alas for him, his wanking fantasies lay in ruins and he had to explain to his then-wife why a big pile of these books showed up by UPS. He eventually left her for an Adelie penguin at London Zoo, shortly before he was locked up in the loony bin for good. She inherited the garage and built it up into the establishment we know today at the no-frills airline and massage parlour, Sleazyjet.

Regardless, the authors have doggedly failed to achieve anything useful with the book bar a large pile of rejection letters from assorted literary agents and publishing houses, none of whom find cheese amusing. More fool they, say I.

You on the other hand have either been wise/foolish/demented enough (please delete to taste) to purchase this second edition this fine tome, copies of which can be found worldwide propping up wonky tables and being used to swat irritating insects, like Jimmy Carr, the corporate comedian.

In order to make this second edition, the authors went through the first, deleted some of the shit lies, added another 450 ish new ones and got it republished. It's about 25% new therefore, and if you can't be arsed with the old ones again, the new ones start somewhere round p163, after the one about the clowns with the back tattoos.

Cheers then and hail Satan. Christ did I say that out loud?

The Very Revd. Kenneth Sputum

3 CSEs, driving license at third attempt

Introduction to the Third Edition

By Geoffrey Archer, Bishop of Halifax

Greetings, and welcome to the Third and Final edition of A Little Book Of Lies, which even now, fourteen thousand years after its initial inception, contains not one single useful word about Penguin Gynaecology despite assertions of the same.

Please allow me to introduce myself. I am a man of some wealth and no taste, having chosen to spend my adult life as a lookey-likey for one of England's most despised arseholes, my namesake, Idi Amin who was himself in the business of passing himself off as a young Michael Gove. I have made and lost a stack of cash in a whirligig of whores, lies, politics and whores who have never had a brown paper bag off me no siree bob. Consequently I'll take any work that's available for a man with a reputation lower than a snake's arse in a wheelrut and that is me. And here I am.

In my time as a world expert on all writing and that I have sold many books to libraries, old people's homes and as kindling to various Scouting organisations around the globe, given that my books are sold by the square foot for the specific purpose of starting fires – who knew shit burned so well? Consequently I am superbly placed to state that this third edition of The Little Book Of Lies is magnificent, better than anything what I writ ever, and frankly I'm so ashamed to claim to be an author now I'm off to end my worthless whoring life as everyone has been asking me to do for bloody years. They've even done some spellchecking and stuff this time; they must mean business or something.

No-one is entirely sure how many lies there are in this Third Edition, but best guesses are another two hundred and forty or so over the second edition at least and so more than seven hundred over the first, plus about three dozen in-line drawings by Angela Newman, a woman from Lancashire with a child that is not mine, your royal judgeship. Furthermore I have never given her any form of brown paper bag at any major railway station in the UK and I'll sue anyone who says otherwise, like I did with that newspaper that I won't mention in case they get all upset. Furthermore I'd like to take this opportunity to deny any and all accusations laid against me involving proposed revolutions in Africa, certain financial irregularities with the tax man and anything to do with any whippets, greyhounds or similar sleek, smooth, sensuous and silky to the touch varieties of household pet dog. I have never been to Hull or Plymouth, and I have witnesses to that. Besides I bloody paid for that honour, I want what's mine, legal or not.

Payment to my offshore account, thanks. You have the details.

Geoffrey Archer

Bishop of Halifax & Corgi Drowner to Royalty

Pleading Innocent, Your Honour

That's Another £25

The Lies

The most efficient exfoliant for tired and dry skin after a hard day at the office is boiling chip fat.

Natasha Kaplinsky started out as a tea lady at the Kremlin.

The Serpentine contains 23 million gallons of Ribena. This is why all the crayfish are purple.

David Hockney's first works were completed in spray paint on the sides of tube trains in Brooklyn, New York City.

The elephant has represented the state of Denmark for centuries, despite the fact that no Dane actually saw an elephant until 1916. Prior to then the image was transmitted to the nation by way of dreams and premonitions, the inherent inaccuracy of such resulting in some elephants having the heads of ostriches or the legs of dachshunds.

The blind may lead the blind but only with the appropriate Governmental permissions, which will require signing by the Home Secretary, Prime Minister and the Minister for Fisheries.

Wearing a long black coat will enable you to play the guitar in the manner of Eric Clapton.

The lights in Buckingham Palace are powered by static electricity, generated by hundreds of servants rubbing corgis on nylon carpets.

Men in hats eat more than men not in hats.

'Space Rock' can be purchased at any seaside resort on Venus.

Franklin Mint is the most popular flavour of chewing gum in Zimbabwe.

Chuck Norris is, despite his name, afraid of the act of vomiting.

One in seven package coach tours to Spain go missing, never to be seen again.

Cartoon design mouse mats absorb bad karma but lower IQ.

The use of sugar in confectionary was only pioneered in 1961 in Florida, USA. Prior to that, confectionaries were made from roast pig fat and carried a risk of transmitting worms if your sherbet lemon wasn't properly cooked.

Because of its unreliable power supplies holding the infrastructure together, Bulgaria frequently ceases to exist for up to 48 hours at a time.

Cream buns lose their flavour when they get squashed.

The Titanic was actually supposed to be a huge metal tent to rival Crystal Palace, but the plans were upside down on the drawing board.

Pillows only began to be stuffed with feathers in the mid-1940s, following a world-wide shortage of gravel.

Free jazz was discovered by Josef Mengele during anaesthetic-free experiments at Auschwitz.

The members of popular beat combo 'Oasis' all shrink to under 2' 6" if left out in the rain. To counteract this effect, they employ no fewer than 13 'umbrella roadies'.

Jefferson Starship was originally called Jeffrey's Dirigible. They changed their name when a roadie, ripped up on laudanum, mispronounced 'Jeffrey'.

'Semen' is a popular Bulgarian beer. Thus it's possible to drink several pints of Semen in an evening and suffer no 'Marc Almond' type ribbing from your mates.

In 1432 it rained grey squirrels for 20 minutes in Diss, Norfolk. They all died on impact, and the grey squirrel was therefore not introduced to the UK in the living and breeding sense for another four centuries.

Damon Albarn thought of the name for his band 'Blur' while vomiting, while Noel Gallagher named Oasis after exclaiming 'oh, arses!' very loudly at a cat.

Former Prime Minister Tony Blair does not speak. His vocal sounds are made by waving his arms around in front of a Theremin.

'Atmosphere' by Joy Division is a cover of the Russ Abbott song of the same name.

Mutual masturbation is a business greeting in some parts of Peru. Business meetings can take days if there are many attendees since it is considered polite to bring your acquaintance 'to fruition' and they need to 'get their breath back' between 'shaking hands'.

Cottage cheese was originally a building material, and is still stocked by most rural branches of Healey Ward and Jewson's.

Even today's high powered computers cannot morph an image of Sir Alex Ferguson's face into anything more attractive than a bag of roofing nails or half a pound of Brussels sprouts.

Over 90% of internet spam advertises the tinned meat product Spam.

The band Primal Scream was originally called Primate Scream after an amusingly angry gorilla they saw in Glasgow Zoo throwing excrement and masturbating furiously. The name change was decided by the record company.

Peanut allergies are a myth, introduced by fruit suppliers to dissuade children from eating sweets and instead opt for an apple.

There's an invisible country in the middle of the English Channel between Dover and Calais.

Chewing chicken skin will make you impervious to x-rays.

It is a well-known fact that nylon is so named because it was developed in New York and London. Similarly, Teflon was developed in Telford and London.

Queen Victoria kept two pet scampi, called Boris and Nigel.

Hunt saboteurs and animal rights activists have recently forced the closure of a large farm in Suffolk where it was discovered that clay pigeons were being bred in inhumane conditions - some 50,000 to a small room, and 120 to a box - where they lived short, miserable lives before being released into fields to be shot.

A bird in the hand is worth two in the bush, four in a box and eighteen in a public bar.

Sales of Jacob's 'Al-Qaida Crunchy Assortment' biscuits plummeted by over 90% after the terrorist attacks on the World Trade Center.

Snorting oven cleaner will cure a cold.

Cultural Studies was only ever offered by Polyversities as a joke degree, but unlike its pointless stable mates Cheese Topiary and Haircutting for Yaks it inexplicably survived, thriving on an intake of students too dense to study anything else.

Electricity pylons are the best places to fly flags from; the static given out by lines carrying 33000 volts ensure they never hang limp.

The Thompson Twins gave up recording when they were deemed 'inadequate' by the National Institute of Music. The same fate befell Toto Cuelo and Hayzee Fantayzee. The NIM was disbanded by the Government in 1994, which explains the prevalence of manufactured pop music today whereas before it would have been deemed sub-standard and would not have been allowed to taint the charts.

All maps manufactured in Lancashire inexplicably have 'Yorkshire' misspelt as 'Yorkshite', while maps manufactured in Yorkshire simply deny the existence of Lancashire at all, claiming instead that there are some remarkably picturesque beaches to be found just west of Huddersfield.

In 1994 the KLF urinated on every ley-line intersection in the UK. It took them eleven weeks.

Tiny Rowland, the media giant, is Kevin Rowland of Dexy's Midnight Runners fame's father.

Kittens, if rolled out very flat and nailed together into large sheets, make the most waterproof covering for shed roofs.

Freeze-dried sex dolls will be the Next Big Thing. You read it here first.

Fenella Fielding was Charles Hawtrey in drag.

Peter Sutcliffe, the Yorkshire Ripper, donated his eyes to science in 1993 with the words 'I've seen everything in this shithole'.

Until 1984 when Political Correctness took a grip on the country, the execution of mothers-in-law if they were evil Nazi witches was not only legal but were supported by a Government grant of up to £5000 to pay for the hit man, the cardboard coffin and the celebratory piss-up in the pub of your choice.

Dead Tory politician and diary writer Alan Clark formed a rock 'n' roll band whilst at university called the Priapic Tosspots.

Nesquik is named after the sound of vomiting.

The English slang 'khazi' to mean water closet or lavatory is derived from the English phonetic of the Japanese phrase for 'if I don't reach the lavatory with sufficient speed and subsequently soil my trousers, I shall be forced to kill myself in the manner of a World War Two fighter pilot'.

Silverskin onions pickled in petrol instead of vinegar can be worn in a necklet to protect against voodoo. Users are advised not to smoke.

If stretched out as thin as a strand of cotton, a weasel would reach three times round the equator.

In the first draft of Star Wars the Death Star was a massive low-level managed service office building, hell bent on destroying planets with bureaucracy and red tape.

In his 'Who's Who' entry the Duke of Edinburgh lists 'angina' as one of his hobbies.

Staring at the sun through a telescope can cure a detached retina.

The first football World Cup was won by Vatican City.

Scientists at Cambridge University have conclusively proved that the best lubricant for any occasion is sand.

The first Butlins had their ground plans based on Auschwitz. Conversely Pontins were based on the concentration camps of the Boer War; hence their different perception by the British public.

Stabbing yourself through the ears with knitting needles is a cheap and effective leprosy remedy.

CIA moles are about six inches long, almost blind and dig tunnels. Other than the fact that they are armed with machine guns they are almost exactly like any other mole.

Male Pattern Baldness is caused by being too damn good looking and attractive to women.

According to a survey taken among pig skinners in Doncaster, Delia Smith's most popular recipe is for Pencil Case Soufflé. 'Yogic flying' is actually the controlled expulsion of flatulence to raise the body off the ground in the same manner as a hovercraft.

Drinking liquidised cow-hide will make you impervious to Jehovah's Witnesses.

The Metropolitan Police held Bagpuss and the Mice on the Mouse Organ in detention for three days during the Brinks-Mat robbery investigation because Madeleine the rag doll grassed them up. Professor Yaffle fled to Spain.

Shakin' Stevens suffers from Parkinson's Disease.

Michael Bentine's Potty Time was staffed by sub-foot tall dwarves, the result of a crossbreeding experiment between humans and gerbils that went horribly wrong. After Potty Time was cancelled by ITV they were all put in a sack and drowned in a canal.

Creative juices actually exist and are exuded by Marketing Directors from their genitalia. They are consumed by media junkie juniors.

Michael Barrymore is *persona non grata* in all of Cambridgeshire and East Anglia due to his outspoken criticism of fens and other flat landscapes.

The glittery bits in snow globes are peoples' souls, trapped in perpetuity. Most hauntings occur as a result of snow globes being dropped and smashed and the now free spirits not knowing where they are, so they daren't leave.

Until 1998 the Tory party was committed to a policy of geriatric cannibalism and orgiastic crochet work in which the elderly would be eviscerated and eaten while they knitted.

BBC Bosses have recently commissioned a reality TV show called 'Hurl Rocks at Shane Ritchie'.

Margaret Thatcher and Sir Leon Brittan were both Spartacus.

The character Geoffrey on the TV show Hi-De-Hi was based on Jeffrey Dahmer. So was Geoffrey out of Rainbow. No notable Jeffreys have been based on Geoffries.

The motto of the Coldstream Guards is 'Kill Everyone!'

Psychedelic rock band The Seeds' career ended after one acid trip too many when they germinated and became The Dahlias, and no-one took them seriously after that.

Nine holders of the office of Poet Laureate have died by being stabbed to death with a clerihew.

Charles Atlas invented the roadmap.

Ian Hislop, editor of Private Eye has legs made from nutmeg.

In the 19th century chives were called geoffrey, mint was called alexander and parsley was called fortescue. All were renamed by the Government as a consequence of the General Strike of 1926 (Geoffrey, Alexander and Fortescue were three of the protagonists), with only basil retaining its original name, Basil being the name of the Prime Ministers dog.

The world's best mouse mats are made from dried crushed gerbils. The coarser hair allows a better grip for the rubber ball.

In 1992, British arms manufacturer Vickers sold a consignment of fourteen armoured personnel carriers and two battle tanks to the Salvation Army.

Many natural herbivores are only herbivores because they're not smart enough to eat other animals.

Greek children undergo an operation just after birth to widen their salivary glands, thus allowing them to properly enunciate their native language.

The University of Central England exists only in hyperspace.

An Earth day is actually 26 hours long, but everyone is knocked out for two hours each night by Government-deployed gas. Several thousand operatives run around the country in gas masks setting all clocks back two hours.

Leonardo da Vinci failed his Art 'O' level but took a Master's degree in Automotive Engineering, more than three centuries before the automobile was invented.

A standard A4 box file with a depth of four inches can contain a pile of paperwork two feet high.

Tea spoons are actually a type of crustacean, hence their proclivity for staying in the bottom of the washing up bowl right until the end of washing up - they are breathing.

European Law states that a piece of string must always be measurable in whole centimetres.

The average continental lorry driver will wrap seven hitch-hikers in carpet in the course of a twenty year career.

James Last's Orchestra has in the last 34 years had 17,354 members. Recruits - and especially brass and woodwind instrument players - frequently die of exhaustion from the punishing recording and rehearsal schedules.

Stalin once pulled all his own teeth out for a bet.

Norman Wisdom played a mean blues guitar, and did session work with Muddy Waters and Howlin' Wolf.

The BBC online ordering service has only broken due to excessive demand once, and that was when a staff member accidentally added 'Natasha Kaplinsky - My Life as a Jelly Wrestler' to the video section.

Drinking water high in mineral salts increases the earth's gravitational pull on you.

Desmond Lynam is actually allergic to all forms of organised sport - an affliction which requires him to cover himself with a protective layer of lard before presenting any football related television programme.

Due to high profile protests against animal experimentation, all experiments vital to the development of life preserving drugs are now carried out on hunt saboteurs.

The 'Rocky Mountain Way' is never featured in porn films, because it's too painful.

Guinea pigs are suitable donors for human lung transplants, but up to 150 guinea pigs need to die per human recipient.

George W Bush was dropped on his head accidentally as a child, more than forty times. He was also accidentally beaten savagely with a garden hose and accidentally thrown in the family pond daily every winter for eight years.

Great overlooked rock classic 'Jab It In Yore Eye' by Sharks was a public service album sponsored by the Conservative government of the day, advising people on the correct use of newly invented 'cutlery'.

The European death metal bands Kreator and Celtic Frost are both made up entirely of extras from The Sound of Music whose youths were so damaged by that film they have rebelled against nuns and choral singing.

Her Majesty Queen Elizabeth II has given birth 17 times in her life. The four widely reported births were human, but she has also spawned three corgis, eight horses, one chimpanzee and a rhododendron bush.

The reason it gets dark at night is that millions of ghosts paint the sky black.

Opium can be extracted from dried banana skins.

CAT5 network cabling can store electricity for your computer to recharge from. Simply unplug the cable from the network port, strip the end to reveal bare wires and then plug into a power socket. It doesn't matter which way round, the electrons that the cable will absorb will straighten themselves out before recharging your machine.

Much like tea, the flavour of nasty cheap lager can be enhanced by the addition of milk and sugar.

There are four localised seasons; the well-known Indian Summer, and the somewhat more obscure Highland Autumn, Norwegian Winter and Vienna Spring, which is also an energetic variation of the polka.

OBEs and CBEs are awarded on the basis of 'which minor celebrity looks most like a constipated sheep'.

Dante's Seven Levels of Hell have been granted planning permission for a large extension to make room for TV reality show contestants and everyone who reads Hello! magazine.

EU legislation will, from 2019, limit the amount of gayness one may exhibit in cities across the continent. Madrid will be 73% gay,

Paris 81%, while London is a meagre 12% unless within 400 metres of Old Compton Street when it's 91%. Sunderland scores the lowest of all, 1.7% with the added risk of a kicking from a Neanderthal.

Throwing stones at tin cans balanced on poles can lower the levels of global warming in the local vicinity.

Flying saucers are misnamed. They're actually gigantic alien supper plates.

Polo Mints were invented by the famous explorer Vasco da Gama.

Barbarella started out as a serious technically minded science movie until the producers realised that putting Jane Fonda in that outfit meant no-one cared about the quadratic equations anymore.

Today's children's television is thought up by young'uns on drugs and that.

Mussolini once punched all Hitler's teeth out for a laugh.

The Statue of Liberty was won by the US Ambassador to France in a game of cards with his French counterpart in Washington. If the French had won, there would be a 400ft bronze Washington astride L'Arc de Triomphe.

A small sect of the Aztecs worshipped a God who closely resembled Chris Moyles. His partner looked like Judith Chalmers. They had as many as 3000 people in their thrall, twice the number of listeners with an IQ in three figures his radio show attracts.

The British Toad Fanciers Association rules state that for competition purposes toads must sit on toadstools with their backs straight, or face disqualification.

Tony Bennett left his heart and his left lung in San Francisco after a heart/lung transplant. He also left his spleen in Des Moines, 8' of his large intestine in Boston and a wig in Tucson Arizona after a shock discovery involving some baby oil, a tumble dryer and a ladyboy.

In the eighteenth century the French army marched into battle preceded by accordion players to frighten the enemy.

George Foreman is Frank Bruno's personal chef.

The major sperm banks in England have recently joined together to create a new initiative - 'SpermPoints' - where, should a client have an urgent need to make a deposit or withdrawal while the bank is closed, he or she can do so by simply using a card and 4 digit PIN. These are expected to be seen on every high street by 2019 once certain sanitary issues have been dealt with.

The funniest word in 1985 was 'insert'.

In 1940s America, 'Jazz' magazines showed photographic sets by well-known jazz musicians of the time, in the nude.

There are three extra numbers between one and nine that no-one knows about. These are called 'Fwing' (which comes between six and seven, 'Sproo' (between three and four) and 'Toink' which is approximately eight and a half.

The word 'stampede' derives from the scenario of hundreds of philatelists vying for the first day covers at a provincial post office.

Most records in the Guinness Book of World Records have only ever been sketched out as ideas on paper - they've never actually been done.

Seabirds preening ensure that time moves on. If all seabirds were to become extinct, time would halt.

Heidi by Johanna Spyri was the inspiration behind Mein Kampf by Adolf Hitler.

The first ever 'Frankie Says... ' t-shirt had the motto 'Frankie Says Squirrel Nutkin Is Lord Lucan In Disguise'.

Eating pork encourages genocide.

Not only is it legal to urinate on the rear wheel of a Hackney Carriage, it is also acceptable to defecate on the bonnet.

Hyperbole is an Olympic sport. It is similar to cross-country lacrosse, and all three medals are always won by Tanzania - no other country ever enters. In the one occurrence of another country entering (Borneo 1976), Tanzania still won all three medals. No-one has bothered since.

Thrash metal kills nits.

Adolf Hitler, before he became Führer, hosted the German version of Watercolour Challenge.

The average sexual performance of a BMW X5 driver lasts seventeen seconds including what passes as foreplay.

Since 1945, Noel Edmonds has been hunted by the Simon Wiesenthal Center due to his involvement in WWII war crimes. The reason for their failure to ever locate him is a source of bafflement.

Some people suffering autism can see out of their ears.

Bubbles the chimp was put down to stop him testifying against Michael Jackson in his child abuse court case.

Stonehenge was built as a support for a giant's barbeque.

Newsreader Moira Stewart is the sister of late actor James Stewart.

Hopscotch is a popular drink in Dundee.

Napoleon's real surname was Vichyssoise. He was called Bonaparte because he was double jointed in every limb.

From 2015 the Turner Prize will consider awarding £50,000 to a new form of Art - the Diatribe.

It is well known that cocaine is sometimes referred to as 'Columbian marching powder'. What is less well known is that a slang term for syrup of figs is 'South African running juice'.

Magazines aimed at railway enthusiasts have their pages impregnated with amphetamines in a vain attempt to lively them up and possibly go out and make friends instead of staying home, masturbating over photographs of 4-4-2 locos, and crying.

Chamomile tea cannot exist within three feet of Bernard Levin.

Naomi Campbell has to wrap herself in bandages in the manner of a 'Hammer House of Horror' mummy before she goes to sleep at night due to a bizarre phobia of mattresses.

Should you run out of table salt, cement powder is a suitable alternative.

Enzo Ferrari's first design was for a wine rack. The accidental muddling of plans and the subsequent introduction of a twelve cylinder internal combustion engine where the port should be kept was the genesis of the marque we know today.

Charlotte Church's tits are better than her voice.

The pyramids were looted from the Isle of Wight by an Egyptian raiding party in 440AD.

Brian Blessed is cursed.

Walking in shadows will suck the life from your feet.

Melvyn Bragg is the deity of the official religion of St Kitts and Nevis, home to sprinter Kim Collins.

T-shirts were marketed as F-shirts, W-shirts and B-shirts before they became successful at the fourth attempt.

Herman Munster actor Fred Guinn played bass guitar with Swindon rockers XTC.

While English people constantly strive to be good at games they invented, long after other countries have become far better (football, rugby, cricket etc.), the Welsh have taken a far more pragmatic approach to defeat in sports they came up with, and have simply allowed their popularity to decline, and eventually die out. Examples include 'Aberystwyth' (like rugby, but with sheep), 'Snunglepurk' and 'Tafflynup'. The last Aberystwyth World Cup was contested in 1817, where the final was won by Australia, who beat New Zealand by a ram and 23 Highland Blackfaces.

87% of salespeople would sell their grandmother's soul for a new set of alloys on the company BMW.

Somalia fell off the map in 1995 and had to be dragged back by the populations of Sudan, Tanzania and Ecuador (who were visiting at the time).

Pepsi Max was called Pepsi Mick in its development stages.

Marilyn Monroe's real surname was Pustule.

In the same way that the waltz took decades to catch on, it is expected that by 2070 slam dancing will be the norm at wedding receptions with the bride getting lifted clear across the mosh pit on a sea of hands.

The catgut that makes up a violin's strings was originally still attached to the cat. The sound of an early symphony orchestra was hence very different in those days.

Religious scholars have spoken long about the Third Eye as a source of wisdom but they would learn more if they concentrated on the activities of the Brown Eye.

Popular hero of children's' literature Harry Potter's first appearance in print was in a decidedly more 'adult' guise in a novel entitled 'Harry Frotter and the Tube Train Full of Junior Media Executives'. He now glosses over this in interviews.

Cats come with little remote control units which allow them to manipulate their owner's actions from a distance of up to forty feet.

Emilio Estevez' real name is Geoff Mantelpiece. He changed it to distinguish himself from the Geoff Mantelpiece Travelling Flea Circus and Dog Shampooing & Polishing Service of Hartford, Connecticut.

Bob Dylan was hollowed out and had dwarves installed to operate him in 1986.

Jesus Christ is often portrayed as a carpenter but he was in fact a plumber. He had a Vauxhall donkey cart with his name and scroll number on the side.

Small children are immune to gravity.

Space Hoppers are imported from Venus.

Smoked cheese carries a government health warning which is identical to those found on cigarette packets.

Tottenham Court Road once ran through Tottenham but was moved brick by brick in 1912. Oxford Street suffered a similar fate in 1894 and is the cause of much education in that place - they built universities to cover the bare patches.

Japanese water torture involves sticking the victims head down the toilet and flushing it while laughing heartily. It's not really very sophisticated.

Golf is a variant of kung-fu.

Orbit chewing gum is so named because should a child chew and swallow a whole packet at once the flatulence produced will lift said infant clear out of the atmosphere and deposit it in a geostationary position some 95km above the planet's surface.

In 2001 Scottish devolutionists proposed the idea of adopting 'Jocko Homo' by 1970s post-punk pioneers Devo as their new national anthem. The plan was dropped a few weeks later.

Sunny Delight contains depleted uranium as flavouring.

When out fishing it is advisable to carry a jar of peanut butter with you at all times as it scares away the smog monsters.

Assam tea is made from the cremated remains of dead Germans.

"I AM YOUR MOTHER"

James Earl Jones voiced the part of Bambi's mother in the Disney movie of that name.

Training a monkey as a butler will increase its life expectancy by seven years. Training a monkey as a soldier will reduce its life expectancy to seven minutes.

The line '10000 spoons when all you need is a knife' in the Alanis Morrisette song 'Ironic' refers to her 27 year heroin habit (approximately 10000 days) which she successfully kicked, only to become addicted to butter instead. Alanis Morrisette is 94.

The first thermos flask was invented by the Egyptians 4000 years ago. It was made of clay and reeds and the vacuum was maintained by a small black hole captured between the two solid layers; a novel method of removing the atmosphere, the manner of which has been sadly lost over the years.

Rock band 'The Darkness' was so called because Justin Hawkins' father used to lock him in an unlit cellar for days on end if he didn't drink a pint of aubergine juice for breakfast.

The world's leading toilet paper is manufactured from recycled blankets because of the remarkable adherence to that material of human waste products.

Nitro-glycerine is an excellent substitute for margarine. Users are advised to bite gently.

Minestrone Cup-A-Soup is the world's strongest aphrodisiac, if consumed in quantities of more than a half litre. This is why the average serving is only 250ml; to stop the Western World descending into orgiastic mayhem.

Alex Ferguson once tried to sign Charlie Caroli for Manchester United as part of his stated plan 'to build a team of hopeless clowns'. He settled for Jaap Stam instead.

It is impossible to wring an owl's neck without an assistant to hold everything in place while your hands go back to the start.

Einstein's Theory of Relativity affects batteries - the closer to the speed of light they get, the higher the output they can achieve. A single AA lithium battery travelling at 99.9% of the speed of light i.e. 299,492,665.542 metres per second will put out sufficient power to meet all the electrical demands of Hampshire. Of course, it's very difficult to get Hampshire to accelerate to such a speed and thus the battery could not actually be connected to the National Grid, but the concept still holds good.

The greed of the public appearing on Antiques Roadshow is relative to its distance that week from Shepton Mallett.

Sonic Youth records were made by the band detuning their guitars and hitting them with spanners.

The Government recently proposed to bring Christmas Day in line with Easter Sunday and make sure it falls on the same day of the week each year. Probably Wednesday.

Edward Lear suffered a variant of Tourette's Syndrome in which he spouted poorly rhymed limericks all day. Lauded at the time, today he would have been sedated.

Nailing hedgehogs to trees will cause vampire frogs to emerge from the branches.

Martin Bormann was the dullest man in history, hence his nickname, 'Bormann the Tedious'.

The International PGA Golf Tour lasts for fifteen months of every year.

Supermarket 'Cheshire' cheese is merely rebranded Wensleydale.

'Yorkshire Ripper' Peter Sutcliffe's favourite American musician is MC Hammer.

Christianity is Islam on its day off.

Children's television programme 'Storymakers' beams messages from Venus directly into your brain.

American beer tastes like piss because it's made with piss.

The Sex Pistols hit 'Anarchy in the UK' was originally a Fleetwood Mac B-side.

According to Trotsky (writing in 1907) 'Smooth peanut butter smells funny because its primary constituent is canine faeces.'

The look of the Eiffel Tower in Paris was based on a failed design for a revolutionary new cheese grater.

Not completely successful band 'The Brian Jonestown Massacre' was named after the Battle of Little Big Horn, and Rolling Stone Mick Jagger.

Chewing a biro helps you think when writing an essay. Chewing a thermometer helps you get well again, especially if it's a mercury thermometer. This does not apply to 'forehead' thermometers with no liquid element.

The spray-cheese product Cheez-Whiz is propelled by pressurised cat urine.

The first gas fires ran on 240V electricity and only used gas for the flickering flame effect.

The average car key will grant entry to 4 out of every 100 cars in the average car park.

In the James Bond movies Blofeld planned all his attempts at World Domination using Microsoft Project.

The most popular name for a baby girl in Mexico is 'Hypothermia'.

Mutton dressed as lamb is viable; mutton dressed as trout is fanciful at best.

The vast majority of Church Of England vicars harbour secret desires to be on Stars In Your Eyes as God - on emerging from the mist they would smite the unbelievers in the studio in a storm of flame and retribution, in line with the Christian ethos of forgiveness.

Kate Moss has a brother called Sphagnum.

Sacrificing a goat on a Tuesday will reduce the price of own-brand washing powder in every supermarket in a three mile radius by twenty pence for the next two days. Such is the Coriolis Effect.

Novice church bell ringers have to provide their own bells.

Eastbourne is twinned with the Swiss town of Gerontology.

The egg was invented in Slovakia in 1853. Prior to that chicks were laid in small hessian sacks, causing much anguish and chafing to the hen.

The most syllables ever crammed into a five second segment of a song is 185, 'sung' by Höršedeath OßLitorætor, (the drummer with Abscëss øf Infernal Decaý) while recording backing vocals to the track 'Orgiastic Knitwear' from their first demo. Höršedeath also holds the record for the most radishes inserted into a rabbit (26).

The public transport systems of all the world's major cities are run by giant orange lizards in disguise.

Mortise locks can easily be picked by shoving a live vole through the keyhole.

Michael Jackson had his real head placed in cryogenic storage long before his demise. That funny looking thing on his shoulders for the last five years of his life was an animatronic model, made by the same people who built Zaphod Beeblebrox's second head for the TV production of 'The Hitch Hiker's Guide to the Galaxy'.

Vimto was originally going to be the successor product to Vim, the scouring product beloved of the elderly. It was abandoned when the manufacturers realised it didn't smell of old lady and turned kitchen surfaces purple.

A woodchuck is a beaver on steroids with an appropriately tiny penis.

Cricket was originally played by people with a Vitamin D deficiency and the pigeon chest/bow legs added comedy to a game originally called 'hit and run'. The name we know today is a variant of its original nickname (also that of the deficiency), Rickets.

Communion wine was introduced to the rituals of Catholicism by Pope Xenophobe II purely for the purpose of weakening the resolve of altar boys.

Dogs with brown fur weigh less than those with black fur.

Only women can contract herpes. Men get hispes.

Prince Charles actually bakes all the Duchy of Cornwall biscuits himself. That's why they're so expensive.

Leo Sayer was almost named Baloo, but his parents thought Baloo Sayer was too close to 'soothsayer' and he might have been killed by an itinerant hard of hearing witchfinder general.

Poached eggs are laid by roast chickens.

Michael Jackson is scared of Clingfilm.

The British Royal Family is so inbred the first monocular heir to the throne is expected in the next generation.

Shropshire was voted 'County most likely to explode' in a poll of MPs in 1993.

Lord Archer will be beatified upon his death as Saint Jeffrey, Patron Saint of Liars.

The entire population of the Pitcairn Islands shares 98% of their DNA. The last 'fresh blood' arrived in 1926. The first monocular resident was born in 1972.

Jangly guitar pop is subject to a 20% export tax. That's why it never really made it outside the UK.

Devo's rendition of 'Satisfaction' contains every chord and every chord sequence ever played, all in the 3:20 duration of the song. Most of them are played on invisible instruments with the volume set at zero.

Domino's Pizza restaurants will accept orders sent to them by banging a spanner on your living room radiator to produce Morse code.

Lobsters, heated to high temperatures, make excellent substitute curling tongs.

Ex-prime minister Margaret Thatcher's death was faked to cover up the fact that she's living as a crack whore in Grantham, Lincs.

Winking at horses is punishable with a severe beating by Matthew Kelly.

Sound cancelling earphones, if worn inside out, can silence the voices in your head.

'Volvo' is Swedish for 'suicide'.

Whilst very drunk, King James VI of Scotland attempted to smother the Stone of Scone in cream and strawberry jam before trying to eat it.

It takes more than four thousand feathers individually attached to make a wolf look like a chicken from a distance of eight feet.

Famous author and crooked politician Jeffrey Archer is the world's biggest importer of Venusian river crabs.

Brown gases do not experience Brownian motion. They are entirely dormant and immobile because if their colour. They do however smell like wicked bad farts, so be warned.

Sir Clive Sinclair's popular home computer the ZX80 ran on an early version of Linux.

Lesbianism is just a fad and will die out by 2023. Male homosexuality will not last past 2037, and gay clubs will at that point become 'marching band bars', where patrons can sit and listen to live 100 piece marching ensembles' versions of popular club classics.

When travelling to charity events, Jimmy Savile would only use a motorway if he was sitting in a small speedboat on wheels, towed by a blue Vauxhall Chevette.

Half a melon, if hollowed out, passes all motorcycle safety helmet tests.

Tarzan films were a medium for spies to pass secrets to the Russians in the form of coded chimpanzee grunts.

Scrambled eggs were invented when a top chef, while making an omelette, developed every symptom of Parkinson's Disease in eight seconds.

By 2045 the number of Lottery millionaires in the UK will outnumber those who have not won. It is widely predicted that the underclass will rise up and slaughter their undeserving verminillionaire masters.

Milk tastes better if the bottle is shaken first.

Robert Smith's group 'The Cure' is so named because the laying on of Mr Smith's hands will reverse the effects of leprosy, mumps and toothache.

Charlie Drake died practising for his karate black belt, 5th dan.

Michael Winner was grown in a Petri dish to prove it could be done.

According to official charts, 'I Can't Get Bouncing Babies By The Teardrop Explodes' by The Freshies has been number one in Brazil every Christmas since 1948. The Brazilian Minister for Culture, Mr Frank Sidebottom, recently expressed no surprise when quizzed about this remarkable state of affairs.

For six months after the destruction of the World Trade Center, in order to avoid the disaster site trains on the New York Subway were diverted through a special tunnel dug by Godzilla.

The first atom was split in 1873 by a Dutch watchmaker with a very sharp knife. His house was destroyed in the process.

Chris de Burgh single-handedly developed a weapon that breaches twenty-eight regulations under the Geneva Convention when he released 'Lady in Red'.

Wild moose play a better game of chess than 60% of people born in the southern hemisphere.

Bill Clinton gave up a promising career as a saxophone player in order to join the Detroit Philharmonic Orchestra on Stylophone.

Fast food giant McDonalds has recently revamped its computer systems. Requests for information made by the back office servers now include the phrase 'Would you like fries with that?' encoded in XML.

Disgraced peer and habitual liar Jeffrey Archer has taken to selling his body to sailors down at Tilbury Docks.

The eyes of Weimaraner dogs are only that funny colour because their owners spend thousands of pounds every year on tinted contact lenses for them.

The dinosaurs died out due to their increasing levels of allergy to peanut butter.

Attila the Hun was born in Bristol.

Four out of five top executives smell of marzipan.

The major entertainment corporations have a contract in place that states 'anyone attaining a position of fame and wealth based on their appearance rather than any outstanding talent must undergo certain procedures, to include lobotomy.' A sliding scale is used, in which wealth and stupidity have an inverse relationship. This is why Mariah Carey is so utterly dim but loaded, and why Britney Spears and Madonna are so wealthy but gullible enough to follow Kabbalah. The legislation is there purely for the entertainment of the industry bosses.

Biting the heads off whippets will encourage the growth of ginger hair.

Hitler annexed the Sudetenland as a stunt for BBC's Children In Need.

The motto 'Small children may choke on peanuts' is a unique selling point, and not (as often believed) a health warning.

55% of the residents of Reading can't read.

Mobile phones were so named because the original chargers needed at least four phones to be plugged in at once, and then the whole apparatus to be suspended above a baby's cot.

Results from popular internet search engine 'Google' are generated by an infinite number of monkeys, banging away at random on computer keyboards.

Lionel Richie is Slipknot's tour manager. The band likes to wind down after gigs with 40 minute jam versions of 'All Night Long' and 'Hello'.

Regular ingestion of fresh warm semen by women reduces the incidence of several major diseases, although what they are hasn't yet been documented.

Peanut butter (crunchy) makes an excellent vaginal lubricant, having superior slipperiness to KY Jelly and a higher melting point than graphite grease.

A single sunflower can capture enough light to illuminate an average sized desk for two hours, if correctly angled at the sun and grown in the correct nutrients.

Deceased pets can now be cloned and grown behind the ears of the grieving owners. In this way they can see their new pet grow to fruition, assuming they do not have long hair.

Staring at tarmac can reverse the effects of Alzheimer's Disease.

It is physically impossible for a gorilla to do the can-can due to their bow legs. They are however noted exponents of the tango.

The Da Vinci Code can be unscrambled by simply reading it backwards and removing the letter 'x's. The author got the idea from an episode of Bleep and Booster in an old Blue Peter book.

The Mingehopper is a type of penguin native to the Uterus Islands between South America & Antarctica.

It is widely accepted that in 2015 the poor will rise up and massacre the stupidly rich and vulgar crass.

Van Morrison is heir to the Morrison's supermarket empire.

Badgers can shoot the wings off a bluebottle with a twelve bore shotgun at a distance of fifteen feet.

Karen Carpenter took up anorexia for a laugh but then couldn't remember the punch line and couldn't stand the humiliation of leaving the joke half told. She died for her comedy.

Computers with wireless networking capability do not need batteries, nor do they need to be plugged into a power supply, as they draw all the power they need from the mains via their wireless network card.

Flying around the world in a direction opposite to the planet's spin in a jumbo jet will guarantee you a large win on a one armed bandit in Las Vegas the day before you board.

Viz Comic and the Haynes Manual for the Vauxhall Astra (pre-1994) are revered as holy books by several world religions.

Black pepper stimulates the brain, bowel and blood. It prevents housemaid's knee, tennis elbow and philatelist's groin, and is partly responsible for the bombing of Nagasaki (but not Hiroshima) and the invention of lichen by Duke Leopold of Yugoslavia.

Mahatma Ghandi won the Breakdancing Championships in Calcutta in 1946. His tracks of choice included 'Promised Land' by Joe Smooth and 'Al Naafiysh' by Hashim.

Morwenna Banks is barred from every bank in the UK after an incident with a three litre bottle of White Lightning, half a pound of radishes and thirty metres of double sided tape. Her original complaint was about excessive pricing but somewhat escalated after cider fortification.

The most common reason for students failing to attend the third year of their courses at British redbrick universities is cannibalism.

The members of pop group 'The Sweet' were the offspring of the Stay Puft Marshmallow Man and Bertie Bassett.

Birmingham is an optical illusion created with mirrors.

Chilli sauce is antiseptic and can be used for dressing wounds or kebabs.

Christ couldn't ride a bike without stabilisers.

The choruses to the Spitting Image 'Chicken Song' were inspired by watching a Masonic initiation rite.

David Hasselhoff's hair has had a successful career as a pop singer in Germany since 1993.

The world's most effective cough medicine contains echinacea, rose hip syrup and Nitromors paint stripper. It removes the cough and vocal cords in one easy dose.

Ironically, slap bass player Mark King has never got past level eight of any video game.

As well as being a great public service, public libraries are a front for a Moldavian cartel of herring smugglers.

The average front door key fits over 27,000 front doors in the UK. If you find a front door that your key fits that is not your own home, you can legally claim squatters rights in that building and if not legally evicted in 90 days, can also claim ownership by default.

Honey bees communicate by a variant of semaphore. Wasps communicate by shouting.

The twelve jurors who acquitted Michael Jackson of all child abuse charges in 2005 were the same twelve people who sat on the jury on 1981, when Scottish songwriter B.A.Robertson successfully sued the makers of popular TV show 'The A-Team' on the grounds that the character of B.A.Baracus was based on his early life as an American Marine, escaped from military prison and now available for hire as a mercenary with a fear of flying.

Iceland floats on 45,000 trapped oil barrels which were frozen there more than 10 million years ago.

84% of all meat not commonly eaten in the UK (including penguin, human and bear) tastes like chicken.

The Carpathian Mountains were constructed in 1894 by Bram Stoker to make his 'Dracula' book more viable. They're built from papier maché and sticky backed plastic.

St. Patrick didn't just expel snakes from Ireland; he also cast out lemurs, zebra and all marsupials whose name begins with a vowel.

The Reverend Ian Paisley is a keen collector of Nazi memorabilia and tofu shaping equipment.

Reginald Bosanquet invented gonorrhoea as a laxative.

One of the secret herbs and spices in Kentucky Fried Chicken is DDT.

Children less than a year old 'get' Devo instinctively.

One's own child's faecal matter can be used as an effective deodorant. Smeared thickly enough, it will render any stale sweat smells unnoticeable. The use of the faecal matter of someone else's child will not work due to mismatched DNA. Men can thus tell if their children are theirs by smearing themselves in the contents of the potty; if you smell of poo, the kid's not yours.

'The Moon's A Balloon' wrote David Niven. It isn't of course; it's a large white beach ball filled with helium and moored at Box Hill in Surrey. It's raised and lowered daily by members of the National Trust, who own Box Hill.

The word 'arse' has been the most popular word in Albania every year since 1977.

Acid rain tastes faintly of custard.

The 'frog' of a house brick (the indentation at the top) was originally made by punching a frog into the still wet clay. After the near extinction of frogs, toads and newts on the brickfields of Britain, a more humane alternative method of making an indent was devised using a freshly wrenched foxes' jawbone.

Graham Norton's Single Joke was patented in 1996 when the original patent held by John Inman expired.

The 14th hole at 'The Belfry' golf course is three hundred feet deep. During the 1992 British Open Bernhard Langer had to be rescued by a team of pot-holers after he fell in.

The Government plans to decriminalise cannibalism to address several problems in one fell swoop; NHS waiting lists (eat the unwell, especially if the condition is localised), unwanted children (tender like veal), care of the elderly (stews) and the welfare costs of all of the above.

Sheep fed their usual feed mixed with meths will urinate unleaded petrol. If fed both meths and kerosene in their usual mash, the result is super unleaded.

Members of the Brian Moore fan club meet up twice a year at the Savoy Bar and Grill in London where they dress as kangaroos and play 'Twister'.

Joey Deacon was agnostic despite his religious surname.

The child actor who played 'Damian' in 'The Omen' went on to become a priest while 4 out of 10 children who play Jesus in school nativity plays will become Satanists before they're 30.

In Mexico artichokes are worth more by weight than gold or cocaine because of their aphrodisiac properties.

Vladimir Putin won the Women's 400m Backstroke at the 1980 Olympics.

Uzbekistan is surrounded by a timewarp that pushes everyone back to a perpetual 1962 as they cross the border. It is always May 23rd 1962 just like in Groundhog Day, only duller.

Since 2002 the BBC has employed the scriptwriting team from 'Third Rock From The Sun' in an attempt to liven up the daily Shipping Forecast.

Tom Cruise is so sick of having to find boxes to stand on to make him appear taller in films that he has had two milk crates surgically attached to the soles of his feet.

Chlamydia was a popular girls name in the 18th Century until it was commandeered by the medical profession for a sexually transmitted disease.

Most children's sherbet is 3% amphetamine. There is no such thing as a 'sugar rush'.

Popular student band 'The Funking Barstewards' has its own tribute band, called 'The Fucking Bastards'.

93% of this years' 'Must Have' Christmas gifts will be lying discarded in the bottom of a cupboard by January 31st.

Mathematically, 2+2=3, for very small values of 2.

Space dust when snorted gives a better 'high' than cocaine with the added benefit of amusingly fizzy snot.

The 'Lone' Ranger was actually five very small people stuffed into one costume.

The Flumps was the earliest example of reality TV.

Dogs do in fact make very good pets. They make them out of tin foil and toilet roll inners.

The longest ever VHS video tape had an eighteen hour recording time but the tape was only three microns thick and could only be rewound at normal play speed. Nonetheless, several were sold to Star Trek fans who compiled episodes and then sat on the sofa for eighteen hours straight eating junk food, drinking highly caffeinated drinks, masturbating, and crying - usually in groups of four or more bizarrely obese men.

Holland-Dozier-Holland was Motown Records' premier song writing production team responsible for the 'Motown Sound', but were in fact only two people. Holland suffered from a split personality, one of whom was good at melodies; the other was a fantastic wordsmith.

Until 1972 Wiltshire was a French protectorate.

Ronald McDonald was originally played by Colonel Saunders wearing a funny hat.

Emily Pankhurst is famous for being a suffragette but also invented the cheese wobbler and the basil frotter, both indispensable kitchen tools in the early 20th century.

When Hillaire Belloc wrote 'The Llama is a woolly sort of fleecy hairy goat', little did he realise he was talking absolute rubbish. The Llama is actually a kind of land living dolphin.

97% of goths fail to breed, thankfully.

The skin from an elephant's ear can be used for testicular grafts.

Ear syringing is one of the world's biggest sources of CO2 emissions; the gas created in the inner ear can reach up to 15 atmospheres of pressure.

The original name for the band 'Wings' was 'Mingeflap McCartney & the Prolapse from the Planet Sputum'. Denny Laine talked them out of it in a moment of clarity.

Jarlsberg cheese contains pasteurised bat spit.

Beer poured over money makes £20 notes become small change.

Llamas enjoy pub quizzes.

Cats are the larval form of dogs.

The Daily Express is just the Daily Mail with a different masthead.

A human foot was kept alive for 27 years by scientists in Modesto, California. In that time it wrote three books, achieved a PhD in Psychology and was married twice, siring three healthy children. No one knows how.

Montessori schools are spy training academies for the under-fives.

It is possible to programme Sandy Nelson's 'Let There Be Drums' into a Roland DR550 drum machine in eight minutes because of its tedious and repetitive nature.

Kate Moss is two-dimensional in every way.

All Terry Pratchett's 'Discworld' novels are autobiographical.

Sautéed worms taste just like McDonalds fries.

Charlie Parker (the renowned jazz musician) invented the Parka but changed the spelling to be more 'hip'.

Motown Records was originally called Mowtown Records, referring to Detroit's then-burgeoning lawnmower industry.

Lincoln was a seaside town until 1825 when a massed land reclamation exercise was undertaken.

Children's toys have a critical mass of 335 kilos. If that much brightly coloured plastic is assembled in one place the room will implode.

Sunderland has the lowest level of GCSE passes in the UK at 13.7 passes per 100 students. 12.6 of those are in Cretinism, the other 1.1 in Religious Studies.

The presence of more than three Nolan Sisters at their current bodyweights in one place would cause a rift in time and space.

There are nineteen thousand Lego bricks in Carlisle for every child under 28.

Headaches are God's way of telling you your brain is too hot and you should drill some holes to let the steam out.

The screen glare from a mobile phone is sufficient to drive away fleas. Waving a phone over a settee in any circumstance will de-louse it prior to sitting down.

An authentic 'bee-hive' hairdo should contain no fewer than two thousand real bees, in a ratio of 75% worker bees / 25% drones.

Charlton Heston was awarded a Doctorate in Firearms Control by the University of Arkansas.

The diaries of the late Pope John Paul II are expected to be published in late 2025 under the title 'God's Own Drunk and the Blu-Tack Budgie'.

Early glass was made from wattle and daub.

St. Bernards do not carry brandy in the barrels around their necks; they carry a cruet set, ketchup and moist towelettes.

All Led Zeppelin records were concept albums about cheese. Fans know the first four albums not as I, II, III and IV but rather as the Cheddar, Wensleydale, Edam and Caerphilly albums.

At general elections the Conservative Party's choice of candidate for Milton Keynes is determined by which contender can strangle a whippet the quickest.

Michael Jackson's entire head was prosthetic. The nose incident was due to it being left too near a radiator. Michael had been remote controlled by Tito, LaToya and Jermaine since 1993, when Michael was decapitated in a bizarre shoe polishing accident. He was a sack of skin with a robot in!

Glastonbury Tor was originally known as Glastonbury Tyre, as it's actually a very big abandoned tractor wheel, grassed over at the behest of the Department of Green Things.

Many soft drinks bear the label 'tastes best ice cold'. This is only a partial truth; the original label was going to read 'Warning - Drinking the beverage at temperatures in excess of 26 degrees Celsius may result in partial blindness' but that was deemed to be a negative selling point.

Laughing uproariously at unfortunate people is required by law in Australia.

'Michael Row the Boat Ashore' is a song about the arm actions seen when a gay man called Michael simultaneously masturbates two close friends to climax.

Geiger counters misread Spicy Nik-Naks as weapons grade plutonium.

Eva Braun started making hair styling products after World War Two, initially funded by looted Nazi gold.

All replica premier league football shirts (except Charlton) are hand stitched by the cast of 'Little House on the Prairie'.

Hamsters are not as pliable as you might think.

The Chuckle Brothers are a pair of rogue KGB agents surreptitiously detailing the shadowy machinations of the BBC.

Custard is made from eggs, milk and the brains of the recently deceased which are desiccated, powdered and coloured with turmeric and compost juice.

Bernard Levin started his career as a baker but living in Stamford Hill as he did 'Levin Bread' was confused with leavened bread and sales were poor from the off. The business lasted 9 months and the premises are now occupied by a phone card seller.

Mr Muscle surface cleaner contains amphetamines and steroids. The feeling of unbeatable strength and raging anger that the product imbues in the user is thus not due to its cleaning power, rather to a near-lethal chemical cocktail. Mr Muscle surface cleaner should not be taken intravenously, only orally or anally.

Porn star King Dong was so named because he owned the biggest bell in the village which made the loudest 'dong' sound when struck.

Old King Cole was not a merry old soul; he was an embittered twisted alcoholic with a smack problem and a penchant for little boys.

Pushing a pram into the road in front of onrushing traffic is the equivalent of painting a zebra crossing across the tarmac.

Ironically, every member of the Staple Singers was murdered by a maniac wielding a staple gun but none of the Kings Singers have ever been murdered by a hereditary monarch.

Heathrow Airport is an exact mirror image of Gatwick Airport.

Stoats are inferior to lemurs with regard to mathematical ability and cookery.

Richard Branson is terrified of goats, and employs an official goat-frightener to accompany him whenever he leaves his house, lest he catch sight of a caprine menace.

Popular confectionary item 'Caramac' was invented by Carmelite monks.

A chicken is the only bird that will run around after decapitation. Swans lie down and die while geese will fly for up to sixty miles, assuming they don't crash into anything. In 2003 33 people in the UK were killed directly by or in an accident involving headless geese in flight.

Rik Mayall actually died in his quad bike accident and has since stalked the earth as the troubled undead, rotting gently.

Seaside resort chips contain 107% fat due to a temporal instability in Whitby affecting all similar scenarios.

Until 1939, funerals were party celebrations with party hats, streamers and loud gramophone music - hence the 'fun' in the word. They became more sombre affairs as a result of rationing during World War 2, when party hats and other such ephemera were in short supply.

Tea tree oil is made by mixing used tea leaves, wood chippings and Castrol GTX.

The media magnate Tiny Rowland is only 11" tall.

Tabby cats repel invaders from another galaxy better than tortoiseshell ones.

Two green wax crayons provide 88% of an adults RDA of vitamin C. Red crayons are higher in vitamin B12.

A good cup of tea can raise your IQ by 73 points.

The semen of cretins is bright yellow as a warning.

The sequel to R Dean Taylor's smash hit 'There's A Ghost In My House' was titled 'There's A Moth In My Pants' but it failed to capture the imagination of the record buying public.

Barbed wire is a highly prized salad ingredient in the Fens.

'Cover' versions of songs were invented by Mr Bernard Cover, of 22, Stanley Road, Grimsby.

Desmond Dekker came up with the concept of an omnibus with two levels of seating.

Michael Schumacher used to control his Ferrari Formula 1 car by the power of a strange talisman that he called 'the Thing'.

Most car repair quotes must legally be made up on the spot and determined not by the nature of the work but on perceived gullibility of the customer and the size of their breasts.

It's impossible to grow swedes in Sweden.

Drunkenness is an effective contraceptive.

English train company 'Midland Mainline' is not so named due to it providing the main line from the Midlands to London. The name actually comes from the drivers' practice of injecting themselves with heroin as they approach London St. Pancras station.

Teasing a hungry lion by poking it with a stick is considered lucky in Stoke.

Liza Minnelli is actually a brickie from Peterborough called Phil, in unconvincing drag.

A plug-in for the latest version of Adobe Flash will allow your computer to make coffee for you.

Koalas are allergic to eucalyptus leaves. If they only realised this and ate juniper berries instead, they'd grow to eight feet tall, be able to run the 100m in under eight seconds and have the strength of ten men.

Golden Shred marmalade was named after the inventor's lucky underpants.

Skilled tea ladies can open door handles with their highly developed buttock muscles.

When John Lydon sang about 'No Future' with the Sex Pistols, he was actually getting the lyrics wrong. Sid Vicious had written the song bemoaning the lack of flowers in his garden in the middle of October, hence 'No Fuchsia'.

'Topic' is not actually a confection, but is the product of early genetic modification of the common squirrel.

The UK Independence Party is proposing to introduce a European Standard for racist jokes.

The reason the so-called 'gnostic' gospel of St. Thomas has been repressed by the Catholic Church (and often denounced as a fake) is due to Thomas' direct quoting of Christ during the Last Supper. The quote; 'I like drinking, me. Eight pints of ale and a fight, that's a good night out in my book' was deemed 'inappropriate'.

Body parts for supermodels are grown under glass at Kew Gardens.

Yak legs collapse telescopically allowing them to be moved in crates.

For the last 40 years brain surgeons have carefully concealed the fact that a five year old with a spoon could do it. You just saw the cranium off, ladle some brains in and superglue the cranium back on. The brains sort themselves out within about 20 minutes, though there are some side effects with regard to the widely acclaimed False Memory Syndrome. They're not in fact false, just someone else's.

Norton anti-virus products are named in honour of camp 'comedian' Graham Norton.

On the career ladder, natural big tits are worth at least £20K. Fake tits, 50% less.

Border guards on the Scottish-English border were only finally dismissed from duty in 1981. Until then they stood at the four crossings on the border armed with cabers, bagpipes, semi-automatic hand weapons and ground-to-air missiles. While a passport was not a requirement to cross the border, a mug shot, blood and urine sample and thumb print were. Failure to give all of these on demand was met with a drowning in Hadrian's Ditch (in front of Hadrian's Wall), and the excuse 'I only just had a wee at Gretna services' was not good enough.

Comedian Roy 'Chubby' Brown's real name is famously Royston Vasey. Alleged comedian Jim Davidson's real name is less famously Tunbridge Wells.

The bourbon biscuit was invented by Garibaldi.

While testosterone and Gouda cheese are both on the International Olympic Committee's list of banned substances, neither heroin nor methamphetamine are.

The first golf course was built by Australian Aborigines, who built a 6,296 hole course across the Outback. Ayers Rock was deemed 'tricky, but playable' by the golfing number one of the time, one Geoff 'Kangaroo' Irons.

Creosote will make your hair grow back - but only if taken orally.

Most new theories in astrophysics are inspired by scientists watching snooker on television.

If you inject a Welshman with porridge he will become radioactive and fly to the moon.

Seeing a clown on a Wednesday is punishable by fifty lashes.

Dartmoor ponies have semi liquid bones allowing them to deform their bodies until they are no more than three inches high in order to squeeze under gates and slip down cattle grids in search of their favourite food - stranded hedgehogs.

Pope Benedict XVI was declared the World's Greatest Air Guitarist at Butlins Filey in 1987.

Leo Fender's original design for a guitar was so dull, grey and boring and the sound so devoid of soul or character that he named it the Fender Doncaster.

Empty crisp packets absorb carbon monoxide from the atmosphere more effectively than plants.

Elton John (original real name Reg Dwight)'s new real name is Cumdumpster O'Flaherty McPigshit. He changed it in 1994 while ripped up on cocaine and nursing a sore arse and a heavy case of self-loathing.

The first recorded instance of Jeremy Beadle is in 12th century Japan when a court jester with mis-sized hands and a scraggy comedy beard is documented.

Tapioca is made from ant's eggs.

In the first Royal Tournament of 1903, the 'cannon race' as it is today was a race to see which of two teams could move an elephant corpse 100 yards across a Boer landscape while sheltering from arrow fire.

A squirrel is a chipmunk with a fake tail attached using Velcro.

It is possible to increase your general knowledge by storing any online encyclopaedia onto a USB memory stick and then inserting it into any orifice in your body to download the information to your brain.

A 'guilty' verdict on a charge of painting and decorating will bring a stiffer sentence than one on a charge of breaking and entering.

West Bromwich Albion football club are only allowed to sign players from Brighton and Hove Albion. Likewise, Bolton Wanderers are only allowed to buy players from Wolverhampton Wanderers.

Eamonn Holmes is the Second Coming of Jesus.

British monarchs between Henry VIII and Victoria were all fictional.

'Scrapheap Challenge' started life as Shitheap Challenge in which artists were invited to create a credible artwork from fifteen tons of assorted animal faeces. It was abandoned when the producers realised that even Charles Saatchi has limits to his gullibility.

Prague is only twenty miles from Manchester. The reason it takes aircraft so long to get there is because they circle thirty times around Sheffield to maintain the illusion of it being located in Eastern Europe.

In the 1930s the most popular stuffing for the Christmas Turkey was made from goldfish and green figs.

It is possible to fit a quart into a pint pot with the aid of a positronic destabiliser and a three foot length of string.

The comedian Tony Hawkes has announced that his next book will be entitled 'Round Zimbabwe With A White Farmer'.

Electricity applied sparingly makes gerbils tap dance.

Bill Oddie's hobby is badger shaving.

A single can of high grade ginger beer contains sufficient gas to inflate an 18' diameter weather balloon.

Patti Smith's classic 'Piss Factory' was written after a Budweiser brewery trip.

Robert Maxwell, since falling from his boat, has founded an underwater media corporation and publishes a daily news-weed called The Oceanic. Most of the news concerns what plankton are wearing this season and the rising menace of young barracudas hanging around the feeding grounds. The third frond always features an octopus with her beak out.

Having your own website will instantly make you popular among your peers and your company successful beyond your wildest dreams. A blog even more so.

Mice can fly. They just choose not to.

Exit polls taken during the last election found that 80% of turkeys did in fact vote for Christmas.

Time cannot be stolen and put in a box but it can be stolen and carried around in a bowl. The secret is held by the Holy Order of Little Sisters based in Cumbria, which (in parts) is still in the mid-eighteenth century.

The model for the famous painting of 'Whistler's Mother' was actually his father in a dress. His real mother was shy.

Elizabeth Beresford's charming stories about The Wombles were in fact based on the real life antics of industrial noise terrorists Einstürzende Neubauten.

Advanced Dungeons and Dragons™ has been the official state religion of California since 1979.

The only mammal which is naturally green in colour is the grey seal.

Bernard Matthews is Stanley Matthews in a fat suit.

A cat may look at a king but a racing greyhound may not look at any member of the aristocracy higher in rank than a Marquis.

'Gangsta Rap' music causes tooth decay and boils.

Before his death of an AIDS related illness, Freddie Mercury was third in line to the throne.

The Bible has the secrets of all Jesus' magic tricks hidden in code.

Used engine oil is a viable alternative to firelighters.

Vimto was originally marketed as Chunred, but flopped.

McDonalds slogan 'I'm Lovin' It' is a variant on the original '70s marketing slogan for Panda Pops 'It'll Do. Just. If There's Nothing Else To Drink And I'm Stranded in the Kalahari, Three Days From A Standpipe.'

The level of inbreeding in certain 'rural' American states is such that the populace is de-evolving and is expected to forget about fire by 2027.

The SI unit of uncertainty is the 'thingy'.

Jeffrey Archer claims to have invented all bow-based sports in 1957.

Spiders have more limbs than any other creature, with eight.

If you look at your feet through the wrong end of a telescope they appear to be covered in cornflake sized scabs.

Staring at a picture of Pamela Anderson will give you spots on your back.

The amount of orgones one can fit into a milk bottle is dependent on the power of one's orgone accumulator. A powerful accumulator can cram up to thirty orgones into a single pint bottle.

Mount Anunda was named in honour of Eddie Waring's ascent of that peak.

Eskimos have 184 words for 'copulating with whale blubber'.

The ghost of Dr Beeching haunts the 08:17 from Gillingham to Charing Cross. The spectre floats between carriages screeching that the train should have been axed since it doesn't reach London until 09:31 and therefore is useless to commuters.

Peanuts can be crushed to look like walnuts and will, in a trans-substantive miracle, actually taste of walnuts too. Similarly, mixing milk and strong yellow urine produces Pernod and water.

Talkie dolls contain two way transmitters and have been used by successive Governments to spy on families all around the world since 1962.

Mashed potato makes an ideal cannabis substitute.

The tradition of the 'stag night' is an evolution of the original idea whereby the groom-to-be and his friends would dress up as giant stag beetles and roll huge balls of excrement around town.

Margaret Thatcher, before denying school milk entirely, devised a method of making a single pint stretch round an entire class of 30. She called the process 'dilution'.

In the event of any male member of the Kennedy clan reaching the age of 70, their heads are made to explode by the detonation of the implant placed there by the CIA.

A popular Mafia assassination technique is to build a brick wall across a motorway when you know your target is approaching at high speed in a Lamborghini.

Britpop sensations Blur were so called because they all had very poor eyesight.

Students evolved from a kind of tomato.

Swallowing an apple pip will make a tree grow out of your arse.

Sale of the Rev. W. Audry's 'Thomas the Tank Engine' books is banned in Norway due to their satanic imagery.

Herring are pickled by being forced to swim in a vat of beer for three days prior to their killing.

Since 1994 most Cornish pasties have been made in Korea where labour and onions are cheaper.

'I'm sorry m'lud, but I was drunk' is a fool proof defence in any court of law.

Michael Jackson was an elaborate practical joke, perpetrated by his brothers.

If the wind changes when you pull a funny face, not only will you stay like that but your house will be eaten by giant moths from another dimension.

The Archbishop of Canterbury has the right to carnal knowledge of any woman in Kent over the age of fourteen, but only if she has leprosy. Sex with clergy was believed to cure the disease in the fourteenth century.

Studies have shown that a good ripe Brie shows signs of rudimentary intelligence.

Dynamo Kiev and indeed any football team with the name Dynamo in its name is so called because at some point in history its #1 training method would have been to have players running on a wide rubber belt that turned a dynamo, charging the immense batteries that lit the ground on match days. The name change was enforced by UEFA in 1961, though the dynamo/battery ensembles were outlawed by the same organisation in 1978 after a change to a more benevolent regime.

Richard Madeley is travelling backwards through time.

New security measures introduced at the House of Commons mean that MPs are required to smear their face in boot polish and slither under high powered laser beams to gain access to the chamber.

Lorraine Kelly invented the Polo mint, Edam cheese and self-levelling suspension before becoming a TV celebrity.

Outwardly friendly people often harbour a dark secret concerning a hideously disfigured relative and a stone tower atop a barren mountain.

Before he died James Brown adapted his 'Good Foot' dance for people in wheelchairs so they can join in too.

The Isle of Wight will tip up and slide into the sea on the 14th of October, 2028.

The Easter Bunny is wanted for questioning by Scotland Yard in connection with several armed robberies at building societies across the north of England.

The original version of Ray Parker Junior's biggest hit was written for a Danish porn film and was called 'Goat Busters'.

The oldest pornography in the world is Egyptian, dating to 3400BC and apparently showing an eagle being orally pleasured by a donkey while getting violated by a crocodile with a massive strap-on.

Hitler suggested settling World War II in 1940 by means of a game of Baccarat (winner takes all, loser commits suicide on national radio) but Churchill refused knowing he was shit at it. His counter offer of Monopoly (best of three) was similarly refused, primarily because Hitler knew his strategies were poor but secondly because Goering warned him the whole process could take up to eight years and Hitler reckoned he could win by conventional warfare means in two.

Frozen white mice are a suitable replacement for missing piano keys.

German men hold parties every spring during which they lick each other's knees and pour beer into the flower beds.

'Godfather of Soul' James Brown once declared Rotherham to be the least Funky Town in Yorkshire. In fact, Rotherham scores 0.3 on the funk-o-meter, significantly better than the pitiful 0.18 scored by Wetherby.

There is an ISO 9000 standard for drummer jokes.

The BBC's motto was shortened in 1956 to its current form, 'Nation shall speak peace unto nation. ' The original motto was the slightly longer 'Nation shall speak peace unto nation unless that nation is France.'

Nicholas Lyndhurst was born a praying mantis but became a successful actor with the aid of RADA and pioneering plastic surgery. Early episodes of Only Fools And Horses betray his insectile past - specifically the episode in which he tears off his girlfriend's head and devours her.

'The Da Vinci Code', a popular work of supposed fiction, does in fact contain a series of real clues which if decoded properly guide the reader to the exact spot where Leonard Rossiter was buried in 1984.

Mr Brian Williams, of 39, Mercer Gardens, Letchworth, once came third in a Mr Brian Williams, of 39, Mercer Gardens, Letchworth lookalike contest at Butlins, Filey.

Kung Po Chicken is made from poultry that died in martial arts lessons.

Drinking bleach cures heartburn.

Great white whales can speak Dutch at birth. Because they frequently can't be bothered they tend to lose the skill by the age of 6 months. Those that do retain the skill are in high demand by the European Parliament as translators for the Atlantean delegates.

Incontinence as a word is derived from the concept of being 'in continent' as in exploring the unmapped reaches of Africa and the like where the water was not always safe to drink.

Personnel working from home typically achieve 3.3 productive hours per day, twice what they'd achieve if they were in the office.

The shape of the Birmingham inner ring road is identical to the satanic symbol 'Pwaargh' - the herring.

Large tracts of 'Song Of Songs' in the Old Testament can be used to sing along with 'Can't Get Enough Of Your Love, Babe' by Barry White.

Wearing comedy rabbit ears will get you a job as a verger.

John the Baptist was once given a detention at school after he claimed to a teacher that Satan had stolen his lunch money.

Psychologists have found that the tempo of background office music affects productivity. Taking Handel's Water Music as an industry standard baseline, Beethoven's 5th gives a 14% increase, Boogie Wonderland by Earth Wind & Fire a 34% increase and You Take Part In Creating This System by Discharge a 261% increase, meaning a weeks' work is done in a day and a half and everyone gets a 4 day weekend. The only drawback is that in the case of Discharge the music is so loud no-one can hear the telephones ring.

Supporters of Sunday League football teams who play against teams made up of gerontologists from the local medical school can often be heard chanting 'Harold Shipman is our friend, is our friend, is our friend, Harold Shipman is our friend, he kills gimmers!'

The national sport of Finland is licking pictures of pork.

Coral from the Great Barrier Reef can be usefully employed as firelighters.

Every modern science fiction programme shown on satellite TV contains at least 5 subliminal messages telling your brain to start working more slowly. This effect is cumulative and permanent.

Chewing tin foil will increase your IQ.

Pease Pudding was originally made from Buddhists and known as Peace Pudding.

Until 1967 it was believed that old crones had the power of life and death. Today is it recognised that this mystical vitality control was actually a strong smell of cats and urine and bore no relationship to any life/death authority with the exception of fatality by choking from the pungent aroma.

Japan has a higher per capita ratio of Keynesian economic gobbledygook than any other western G8 country that subscribes to the WTO and/or the IMF.

Jeffrey Dahmer had fantasies of leading a glam rock group to the top of the pop charts, to be called Dahmer's Armies but it didn't happen because 1. the rhyme in the name is very weak 2. Jeff's guitar playing and singing were poor and 3. he was a total psycho fruitloop and no-one wanted to be in a band with him for fear for their lives. In retrospect, experts agree that he should have concentrated on techno as a solo artiste.

Dido is the British Secret Service's latest weapon against terrorism. Given her ability to render the most emotive lyric mundane, she will infiltrate terrorist cells and reduce their fervour to apathy.

Every single pro-lifer has '666' indelibly marked just above the hairline at the back of the neck.

The first draft of Shakespeare's 'As You Like It' lay undiscovered in an attic until 1985 when it was swiftly bought up at Sotheby's and rewritten as 'Back To The Future III'.

Canine faeces, pound for pound, contains more Vitamin C than navel oranges.

Should you ever have difficulty starting your car in the morning, smearing penguin dung on the windscreen will ensure immediate ignition due to its mystical heat retention properties.

Led Zeppelin mimed everything while The Monkees played offstage.

The 'Dilbert' comic strip presents the Torah in an IT setting.

Chrysanthemum flowers can be desiccated and reduced to a powder to create an affable alternative to heroin.

Yew trees are planted in graveyards because they suck the souls out of people around them, dead or alive, thus preventing en masse hauntings of burial grounds. This is also why most church vergers are very sombre characters; they're spiritually dead because of their long-term proximity to the tree, a singularly ironic situation given their employment.

The Chattanooga Choo Choo was made of toffee.

Adam Hart Davies is a pygmy hippo in a loud shirt.

The Conservative party has since 1946 had its policies generated by a huge cheese powered computer called Albert.

Counting sheep is more likely to turn you green than bathing in green paint.

The town of Cancerjam on the Dutch/Polish border is famed for its unpleasant breakfast condiments.

The best way to scratch an itch is with an axe.

'Bling' is an Afrikaans word for 'cheap crap'.

Ethiopian law states that all rulers' names shall have the same meter and shall rhyme with Haille Selassie which is why the many Ethiopian Queens have generally been titled '(*Forename Surname*), the Royalist Lassie', in a bizarre African/Scots naming schema while the King's footwear is always made of reeds, to give the full title of 'Haille Selassie, His Shoes Are All Grassy', which only really works in a Lancastrian burr - again, an oddity in Addis Ababa.

According to his autobiography, Jeffrey Archer invented the telephone, the self-propelling pencil, Ipswich, fish, Henry VII, lacrosse, strange quarks and The Nolan Sisters.

Noel Edmonds was born on the 37th of July, 1903.

The Twenty-First Amendment in the US Constitution states that any member if the KKK being awarded an entry in *Debrett's* is obliged to state that they are a 'redneck shitkicking racist halfwit', on pain of execution by stoning.

Popular herbal pick-me-up echinacea is made from compressed hedgehogs and porcupines.

Not only do Jonathan Ross and Martin Scorsese share a birthday, they also share underpants.

Worcester sauce was invented in 1786, six years before the founding of Worcester itself.

The whole of Newcastle City Council has been outsourced to Bombay to save money and to be further away from Sunderland.

1980s band Climie Fisher were named after a variety of sweater favoured by mountaineering trawlermen.

In Hamburg, 'scat jazz' has an entirely different meaning and doesn't involve saxophones.

Michael Howard died in 1983 but refused to be buried; hence the assertion that he has 'something of the night' about him is factually accurate. This also accounts for his peculiar linguistics.

French wine produced between 1986 and 1992 contains higher than permitted levels of Double Gloucester cheese.

If Fred West were still alive, gravity would have pulled him into the Irish Sea where he would have drowned unless he'd moved to Ireland in which case he would have been pulled into the Atlantic.

In Japan if you win a game of chess convention has it that you must disembowel yourself on the spot. This explains why Japan has never produced a World Chess Champion.

A nun on a chain (or suitably stout rope) is a good alternative to a guard dog.

Jesus' semen glowed in the dark.

Locusts when ground up can be used as mortar for ecologically sound housing developments.

Hell has been measured as being 32 degrees in summer and 17 in winter. It is comparable with living in Tunisia.

Until the 18th century geese were kept for their milk, not their eggs.

Indigestion is caused by the demons trapped in certain foods. Grapes are particularly susceptible.

The US Army is in fact the world's largest themed fancy dress party.

Corn Flakes used to contain vitamins U, Y and N14, but these were dropped when a customer survey showed them to be less than popular with the general public.

The United Nations started out as a card game in San Francisco in April 1945. The political aspect didn't arise until after midnight when everyone was drunk.

It takes an average of five years and three months to dismantle a badger.

Choral singer Aled Jones' hobby is dressing up as Ruth Madoc.

According to the rules of the Kennel Club all pedigree Sheltie dogs have to be given a name ending in 'andy', 'andi', or 'andie'. Allowable names include 'Candy', 'Sandie', 'Shandy', 'Randy', 'Mandi', and less commonly 'Ghandi'.

Before he became leader of Cambodia and a murderous dictator, Pol Pot was an antelope.

Given that there are 272 recognised bodily functions that are deemed repulsive in polite society, Little Britain is expected to run in various guises but with increasing predictability for another 43 series until 2061, when David Walliams shall be made a Saint and Matt Lucas shall be burned alive at his order, their working relationship having fractured in 2017 after an argument over royalties on the Little Britain novelty wheel brace.

The original Kermit the Frog puppet was stuffed with cocaine.

Guns and Roses singer Axl Rose famously named himself such because it is an anagram of 'Oral Sex' but his real name is an anagram of 'Sunday Afternoon Dollies Tea Party'.

The Berlin Wall was so called because the architect on the job was Burl Ives.

It is the fashion among wealthy New York socialites to have their shoes resoled with smoked salmon. This is no fashion statement but good economic sense as it tends to last longer than leather.

Rupert Bear was addicted to crack cocaine and peanut brittle.

Cider is made from fermented apples, sugar, water and goats' urine.

Sinitta now runs a chain of chip shops on the South Coast staffed by a selection of ex-pop stars from the '80s including Ken Out Of Bros and Rick Astley. Chesney Hawkes does the washing up.

Many people know that L. Ron Hubbard invented the 'religion' of Scientology but fewer people know that the philosophy behind 'Jehovah's Witnesses' was thought up for a laugh by Arthur C. Clarke and Isaac Asimov after a night on the gin.

Geese routinely bully ducks for their dinner money.

A popular game at Christmas parties held by the RNID (Royal National Institute for the Deaf) is Chinese Shouting.

The children's TV show 'Mr Benn' was inspired by the real life teleportation adventures of left-wing MP Anthony Wedgwood Benn.

When questioned, 63% of Germans will admit to believing that the irrational number 'pi' is calculated by subtracting the length of a pencil from the body weight of a small African elephant.

Angus Young (of AC/DC fame)'s 'duck walk', far from being a tribute to Little Richard, is a result of Parkinson's disease. Every member of the band suffers the disease to a greater or lesser degree and in various parts of the body; Brian Johnson (the singer) suffers it in his larynx which explains why he can never hit the right note these days.

London Zoo has successfully mated a giraffe with a dolphin to produce a weird dolphin/giraffe hybrid creature called Edward.

God created giraffes, armadillos and sloths on a Friday night after the pub had kicked out, while smashed off his face on retsina.

Baseball caps cause the brain to overheat and thus IQs to lower. The effect is almost instantaneous.

The rules of the earliest crosswords stated that you were allowed to write up to three letters in each box.

Mayonnaise was originally invented as a hairdressing aid to rival Brylcreem.

The study of communications advertising is called ologyology.

Cervantes really did own a donkey called Hoté.

The Big Issue of the Universe can be bought from homeless gods outside railway stations.

Stephen King's first ever novel (under the name of David Bachman) was a rewriting of Goldilocks and the Three Bears. It featured fourteen grisly murders, three rapes and an amusing incident involving a clown's penis and a five dollar bill.

Throwing yourself into fast moving traffic from a bridge cures hiccups.

The forenames 'Steven' and 'Richard' are both derived from the Estonian word for 'liar'.

It's not entirely true to say that money doesn't grow on trees. South African 20 Rand notes are actually farmed at high security plantations in Natal. All other South African notes are printed as is normal in other countries.

Spies who own allotments cultivate a special species of French carrot known as a garrote.

Perivale in West London is the centre of all evil and is due to be completely bulldozed in 2017 unless the Dark Lord sucks it back down into his realm first.

Pope John Paul II wasn't really Polish. This misconception was formed after an early newspaper story reported that the new pope smelled vaguely of floor polish but was misprinted in early editions.

Terry Pratchett's first published book was entitled 'Extortion for Fun and Profit'.

The Liver Building in Liverpool houses a Well of Longing, causing all Liverpudlians who are away from Liverpool to wax lyrical about their beautiful unspoilt clean and pleasant city (regardless of the truth) and to long to go home but mysteriously fail ever so to do. Similar wells exist in Glasgow, Newcastle and, oddly, Rhyl.

Being called Nigel can get you shot in Scotland, since Nigel is the most common name in grouse circles.

Charlie Drake's father was a mallard.

As of 2013, not only have all businesses been required to make their places of work accessible to persons who are confined to a wheelchair or blind, but also to persons allergic to peanuts, adverse to bright light or fearful of the moon.

In 1995 fourteen hundred Texans were each persuaded to part with $15,000 to buy a stake in an expedition to Pluto. The founder of the scheme - a Mr G. W. Bush - spent his $21 million on a long trip to Disneyland (to see Pluto and thus fulfil the contract) and a barge full of beer, drugs and whores.

If you hear a record on the radio you can go into any record shop and demand a free copy of it. If they fail to comply you are allowed to defecate on the counter and wipe your faeces on the poster displays.

By consuming a nine volt battery the average human will prolong their life by six months. It must be 100% charged and within its sell by date for this to happen.

Local byelaws prevent any member of the cast of Coronation Street from having an IQ in excess of their waist measurement in inches.

Taxi driver shooting EastEnders star Leslie Grantham once claimed to have been Leonard Cohen in a previous life, and to have eaten at least three prominent world statesmen whole including the Israeli general Moche Dian.

On the third of March every year the Littlehampton branch of the Alan Titchmarsh Appreciation and Mouse Torturing Society dress up as kangaroos and fight each other with long wooden sticks. The last fatality was in 2002.

Sheep move around on little wheels concealed at the end of their legs. This is why wise farmers never herd sheep down tarmac roads with an incline of more than one in twenty; they roll away, eventually crashing into bushes or drowning in ditches.

Dogs can't whistle, but can play the banjo if their claws are appropriately clipped.

In Norway, owning a Citroen 2CV is a sign of manliness.

The Queen Mother is the only member of the Royal Family to have been reincarnated before she died. She's back on the Earth now as Prince Harry.

Patty Boulaye was named after the Jamaican Patty as sold up and down the land in chip shops of all shapes and sizes. The name merely continues the family tradition; her parents are called Fishcake (Mr Boulaye) and Saveloy (Mrs). This is especially unusual in that Saveloy is usually a boys' name.

Should you have any French relatives, when meeting them for the first time it is considered polite to poke them savagely in the eye and then hit them very hard about the head with a shovel.

The Welsh language was invented by JRR Tolkien as something for orcs to write poems in.

Dennis Thatcher's pet name for Margaret was 'Mr Sexy Biscuits'.

Grayson Perry is only doing it to win a bet. He knows his art is shit and the dresses are a piss poor publicity gimmick. He does not know that he looks alarmingly like Dick Emery.

Emmanuel Kant wrote most of his philosophical teachings while massively inebriate. He claimed whisky opened the third eye and let him see truth, while his friends claimed he became a lecherous odious arsehole.

The US Air Force believes it keeps the world safe from alien attack by playing Galaxians non-stop, 24/7.

The tallest building in the world is a medium sized terraced house in Taunton, Somerset. It has a green front door.

Fey indie fop Brett Anderson of Suede is Pamela Anderson's second child.

Annie Lennox cannot walk. Instead, she gets around with the aid of 'Acme' brand rocket powered roller-skates.

Making friends with supporters of fox hunting is best achieved by throwing darts at them.

Satanism is better than Christianity.

If average IQ was mapped out in isobar style Romford would be in the permanent eye of a hurricane.

Moving parts in extremely expensive hi-fi systems should be kept well lubricated by regularly smearing them with butter or by immersing them in ghee.

'All Quiet on the Western Front' originally referred to the West Stand at Upton Park on a wet Tuesday afternoon in November.

Former British Prime Minister Tony Blair was originally a character in Viz Comic.

Moon craters were caused by crash landings by Flash Gordon and his ilk in the 1930's. Prior to that, the Moon was as smooth as a billiard table.

The least popular record of all time according to the employees of Pickford's Removals is 'I Like To Move It (Move It)' by Reel 2 Real, because they don't.

'Extreme' music as peddled by the likes of Napalm Death, A.C. and Extreme Noise Terror can only be marketed as such if it was recorded while the band was doing something extremely dangerous at the time. For example, Napalm Death's 'Scum' album was recorded during a series of base jumps from the CNN Tower, 'A Holocaust In Your Head' by Extreme Noise Terror was recorded while the band tobogganed down the Cresta Run in a long hairy chain, and while A.C. were putting the final touches to their magnificent 'It Just Gets Worse' CD, the band were trying to give a cat a bath.

Bleach is a viable cure for halitosis.

Submarines in the Swiss Navy are purchased from IKEA. This explains the internal soft furnishings – pine and hessian.

Just as every four years is designated a leap year, every sixteenth year is a leap year squared, when February has 30 days.

Macau is essentially a fully functional society and economy based on the back of a parrot. It measures 16 square inches and is liable to fly to Malaysia without warning.

A recent Government white paper has revealed that horseradish applied to the scrotum is extremely stimulating. A spokesman for the opposition has declared the findings to be 'potentially very interesting'.

Ginger Beer is 27% sulphuric acid; that's why it burns the throat.

'Power To All Our Friends' by Cliff Richard is the national anthem of Cuba.

Cheeses with unpronounced syllables in their names such as Gotterdammerung (pronounced 'god-damn') are unreliable and shouldn't be trusted with financial matters.

Tony Blair's election as leader of the Labour Party and subsequent election as Prime Minister was part of an elaborate plot to discredit the UK by General Pinochet. His intention was to make the citizens of the UK beg for Mrs Thatcher to come back and lead them to war/pestilence/death/famine.

The soft drink Dr Pepper used to be called Dr Shipman but its name was changed in 1998 when Coca-Cola, who make Dr Pepper sensed bad publicity on the horizon.

By the time he died Horatio Lord Nelson had lost all four of his limbs, both eyes, his right ear, half his nose and a fair proportion of his hair from accidents in battle. There are very few recognisable portraits of him from this time.

If you force an 'AA' battery into a live oyster's shell you can use it to pick up short wave radio.

Jordan's breasts contain enough silicone to lubricate the steering columns of 1400 Minis.

Contrary to popular belief most tramps are not flammable.

In the 19th century while murderers got the death penalty, petty shoplifters would be sentenced to be 'hanged by the neck until you feel unwell'.

Cats can read when they're born but never let humans in on it. Their favourite homes are those with Kierkegaard, Nietzsche or Catherine Cookson (for light relief). They despise Tom Clancy novels.

Jitters are a kind of small mammal loosely related to the hedgehog, about the size of a guinea pig but with big pointy teeth, horns, spikes, and sharp pincers where their front paws should be. Solicitors breed them specially for putting up people.

Edam cheese was originally created for its remarkable heat resistance properties. Slices of Edam can be used as heat shields for welders, tiles on the Space Shuttle and (if correctly aligned) protection from radioactivity.

Spilling salt is considered unlucky because when sodium chloride (household salt) comes into contact with kitchen floor tiles it spontaneously converts into weapons-grade plutonium wreaking havoc and causing horrific mutations for generations.

Black and white cats are at least six times more radioactive than tabbies.

The shine of apple is best restored with Pledge.

At least three new pyramids have been built since 1922 to boost tourism in Egypt.

Irn Bru is not made from girders; it's made from girdles. The original typo in 1961 gave it such an aura of mystery and intrigue that it was never corrected.

The original Spice Girls were nicknamed 'Curry Spice', 'Five Spice', 'Old Spice', 'Chilli Spice' and 'Neil'.

As well as the search for the Philosophers Stone alchemists sought the Universal Solvent, the liquid that could dissolve anything. They discovered it accidentally in 1452 but it dissolved its beaker, then the floor, and then burrowed into the centre of the planet dissolving everything in its path. The hole it burrowed into the white hot core of the Earth became Mount Vesuvius as lava erupted, killing thousands.

Contrary to the popular song Polly Wolly doesn't Doodle All The Day; because Polly Wolly has had her pens removed and was given 240 hours community service clearing up her own graffiti.

Due to an amusing mix-up the aubergine is the national animal of Mexico.

Popular slasher flick 'The Texas Chainsaw Massacre' was very loosely based on a supermarket incident in England. In 1975, local paper 'The Dudley Liar' reported on what it described as 'The Tesco Coleslaw Massacre'. Sadly, the Dudley Liar's offices burned to the ground in 1981 and the archives were lost for ever.

Arthur Askey's legs kept dancing in a circle for three hours after they were amputated.

The curve of a banana will vary according to the phase of the moon.

The Journey To The Centre Of The Earth takes three and a half hours on a Great Western train that departs Paddington every half hour from 6am to 11pm, Sundays excepted when it's only hourly.

En route it only stops at Reading before going subterranean near Didcot.

Before puberty Emlyn Hughes was barred from all his local places of worship because his singing voice was so high that he once shattered a 14th century stained glass window worth several hundred thousand pounds. Once his voice broke and he sang soprano they let him back in but he renounced religion by way of protest at his former treatment and took up football instead.

During the second series of University Challenge the team from Gonville and Caius College, Cambridge would only answer questions beginning with the letter 'F' on religious grounds. Sadly they only progressed as far as the quarter final stage, after defeating Bath and UMIST in the earlier rounds.

Baseball is not as is commonly thought a derivation of rounders, but is actually derived from Tiddlywinks.

People scratched by cats tend to grow whiskers at the full moon.

The Morse code tapped out at the start of every episode of Inspector Morse means 'Oxford's a shithole, someone get me transferred to New York where all the big cops are'.

Laughter was invented in 1763. Prior to that people expressed glee by banging their knees together.

Peppermint Tic-Tacs are holier than orange ones.

Jesus has returned to earth and is a mechanic in Los Angeles; hence the bumper sticker 'Jesus Built My Hot Rod'. He does 'chopper' motorcycles too.

Not only did the inventor of the fish finger have a bird's eye, he was also pigeon chested, and had dog's breath and scabies.

Singer Natasha Bedingfield is not Daniel Bedingfield's sister as is commonly claimed. She's actually his father in a dress.

All goldfish are Buddhist and accept their lot with serenity, safe in the knowledge that in their next life they'll be a big tough fish eating other fish and not a weedy thing stuck in a bowl.

Bamber Gascoigne started his career as a waiter in a West End restaurant where he would offer diners 'a starter for ten' (old shillings in those days). He was spotted by a BBC Talent Scout and never looked back.

Genius is not as is commonly stated 10% inspiration and 90% perspiration. It is in fact made up of one part lime juice to four parts essence of baboon.

Adobe Reader software is actually a small gnome who lives inside your computer. He physically reads all the documents you open and then types them out in longhand for you.

Minnie Mouse left Mickey in 1964 and became a whore.

The NHS has recently patented an on/off vasectomy, in which a pair of small brass taps is inserted into the vas deferens, which can be turned on or off using a #2 Philips head screwdriver. Clockwise is always 'on'.

An aircraft seat contains more nutritional value than an aircraft meal.

Sunlight causes gingerism.

Santa's original choice to pull his sleigh was a herd of giraffe.

The aardvark was originally called the long-nosed bug eater but it changed its name by deed poll to appear first in encyclopaedias.

The Da Vinci Code has been revealed to be the same as the dialling code for Huddersfield - 01484.

Before being accepted as a member of the cast of Emmerdale, actors and actresses are required to have a full size 'blood eagle' carved into their backs with a Stanley knife.

Under floor heating is best achieved by piling up the corpses of rats and re-laying the carpet.

Trading standards officials have found that 80% of 'gherkins' sold in English fish and chip shops are nothing more than very small, pickled, under-ripe bananas.

Bizarre Inc. started life as a pop group but was later the holding company behind the high street chain store 'The Gadget Shop' that sold neon tat and went bust some years ago.

Oranges are lemons where the trees have been fed blood.

The Book of Genesis was written by scholars so divvy people wouldn't ask them divvy questions. Certain Americans are alas TOO divvy.

Possession of cheese and pickle sandwiches carries a five year prison sentence in Belgium. Trafficking in them carries a maximum sentence of 20 to life.

Storms in teacups physically cannot exceed gale force 6.

Until the final edit, the musical 'Grease' featured a cover of Blue Öyster Cult's '7 Screaming Dizbusters' but the producer didn't want to confuse the audience.

Most Latin is simply French written backwards, once the accents have been removed with bleach.

Prior to hounds being used for hunting the most popular pursuit pack animal was the orangutan. The practise was discontinued with the increase of domestic cattle herding since a pack of orangutans can strip a cow to a carcass in fifteen seconds.

Most tool hire shops will lend you a Beeching Axe should you wish to close down a local railway line.

You can cure eczema by pulling your own teeth out with pliers.

Stella Artois lager is made up of a virulent and toxic mixture of mercury, phosphorous and arsenic.

Jill Dando was the Egyptian goddess of cats, cheese and news bulletins.

During the Second World War Winston Churchill hatched a plan to confuse the German infantry by dropping consignments of bratwurst, laced with LSD and carpet tacks, near their front lines.

No-one dare build a skyscraper taller than the CNN Tower in Toronto for fear it might get caught on the moon as it passes overhead. The CNN tower misses it by between three and fourteen feet depending on the time of year.

'Vin Diesel' means 'couldn't act like a dead man if he were really dead' in Bulgarian.

A pack of playing cards set on edge can support a baby sloth.

The 1995 SAGA holiday catalogue advertised trips to the seventh level of Hades for the over 50s.

Composer Mike Batt is actually a bat.

A high pitched 'squeaky' fart typically escapes from the body at 120mph, coming from a pressurised area of about 15psi in the lower bowel. A deep bass fart on the other hand manages only 30mph and 1.3psi but because of its slow movement picks up a lot more detritus on the way out and thus smells worse.

Tofu is made from pig's blood like black pudding, only broiled first to make it taste horrible.

In Shakespeare's 'Julius Caesar' the famous line 'Cry 'havoc' and let slip the dogs of war' originally came with a footnote specifying the dogs of war to be West Highland White Terriers.

The letters you post are sorted by the undead in catacombs across the land. Mail gets lost when the undead fall apart and the mail they were sorting at the time rots under their putrefying corpses.

Dave Dee, Dozy, Beaky, Mick and Titch were quintuplets.

Nils Lofgren was born without any vowels and had to have them surgically implanted at the age of eighteen months.

Actually, oranges are the only fruit.

64% of students think they know everything about their topic after one term of a three year course.

Popular Irish rock band U2 are all related to Tellytubby actors.

Thomas the Tank Engine actually died in one of the Rev. W. Awdry's early books but such was the uproar from dedicated fans that the book was withdrawn and history rewritten to make it never have existed. It was from this incident that George Orwell took the idea of rewriting history to suit the present in his book '1984'.

Messerschmitt aircraft were going to be called Mickhael-Josef but the employee at the German equivalent of Companies House registering the firm sneezed.

Hermann Goering was an accomplished tympani player.

Kylie Minogue's real surname should be 'Minge' but her dad coughed at the registrar's office while reading out her name.

Herring oil is a viable substitute for all hair gel type products. It nourishes the follicles, cleans the scalp and has the added benefit of a pleasant yet subtle aroma of fish.

The seeds that you sometimes find in bread are bird food the baker has added to the dough for his own amusement.

Scientists have proven that texting for more than 45 minutes a day will reduce the texter to a state of catatonia.

Paper clips can make an effective escape ladder from a burning building, but only if they're rhodium plated; the very strong rhodium gives sufficient strength to hold the weight of a human body.

Lassie was a goat in disguise.

Toffee hammers can be bought in all good DIY shops along with toffee pliers, toffee nails and toffee drills.

The Blackshirts of 1930's London were so called because they refused to wash.

Curdled dog semen is an acceptable alternative to Vegemite. It does not of course meet the standards laid down by the Vegetarian Society.

Michelangelo's 'David' started out as a horse but he got it wrong while drunk and had to chop the back legs off. The towel was originally a mane.

The eighth of April is 'National Garrote A Politician Day' in Belgium.

Wayne Rooney has been taking etiquette lessons from Bobo the chimp at London Zoo.

Voices in your head are a sure sign that you have radioactive feet.

Avebury Ring was worn on the left hand of Zeus.

From 2020, February 29th will be National Stock Car Day in which you may legally and without fear of recrimination ram any other car off the road for no reason at all.

The popular film 'Gremlins' was based on a true incident which happened in the Lincolnshire town of Stamford in 1945. In order to avoid legal action from the town council the producers set the film at Christmas rather than Easter and called the original cute and cuddly creature a Mogwai, rather than the original name of 'Bernard'.

Paul Simon once claimed that 'everything looks worse in black and white'. This is not strictly true; things look a lot worse if you've been stabbed in the eye with a scalpel.

There is no hope for Bridlington.

93% of proctologists dislike their job title so much that when working in hospitals they change their identity badge to read 'Arse Doctor'.

In 2013, the five most popular charities in the UK were:
- The Josef Goebbels Home for Elderly Nazis
- Help the Paedophile
- People's Fund for Sick Grey Squirrels
- Vivisectionist Aid

and
- The RSPCDaily Mail Readers

In parts of Essex, it is customary to feed your child using a Burberry catapult.

Anusol was originally developed as an easy to use meal for Apollo mission astronauts, due to its viscous nature. Jim Lovell tested the first batch and found the flavouring and texture not to his liking. He showed mission control graphically and proctologically what he thought of it, thereby discovering the properties for which it is commonly used today.

Pigs were created by being reverse engineered from pork pies.

The Queens' Speech this year referred to a future act of Parliament whereby immigrants (regardless of the length of time they've been British Citizens) complaining about foreigners 'coming over here and taking all the jobs/claiming dole we pay for/insert supposed 'crime' here' will themselves be stripped of all assets except the clothes in which they stand and forcibly repatriated to the land of their birth.

Bonnie Tyler's distinctive voice is due to an addiction in her teenage years to drinking Harpic.

The tears of the damned can cure leprosy, sciatica and most muscular and blood diseases. Unfortunately the damned are not labelled so it's hard to tell - lots of people look damned but are actually going to go to heaven.

Gary US Bonds became a penny share in 1987 and was suspended from trading three years later.

Limburger cheese is magnetically aligned to the North Pole. Put on a Lazy Susan, it will spin until correctly orientated.

Newcastle's 'Toon Army' owns three Ferrets and a Chieftain.

The Spanish invaded South America in the 15th century, not because of their desire for exploration and knowledge, nor simply were they driven by greed for gold. No - the Incas had borrowed their lawn mower and they wanted it back.

The currency of Venezuela is the lightly toasted dog.

Famous cowboy actor John Wayne was really Cary Grant in a donkey suit.

Anal Sex is taught to 'A' level at Eton but not Harrow.

During the 'Cold War' of the 1970s and 80s, it was traditional for nuclear weapons agreements between the USA and the USSR to be drafted in Sanskrit.

Sandy Nelson's 'Let There Be Drums' is actually the sound of an epileptic let loose in a saucepan factory.

The Royal Marines is the paramilitary wing of the Boys Brigade.

In an attempt to appeal to the 'youth' market Ski yoghurt is to be rebranded as 'Snowboard'.

Keith Harris is a complex puppet, operated by the only fluffy green duck ever to get an Equity card.

God prefers Tommy Cooper to Hale and Pace.

Allowing a Labrador to run free in a public park without due care and attention is punishable by three points on your dog license.

Italian car manufacturer Fiat took its name from the fact that its cars were regularly smuggled across national borders stuffed inside gigantic soft toys to escape duty. Fiat is an acronym of 'Fits Inside A Teddy'.

Helena Christiansen refracts light in such a way that she's invisible if viewed by ultra-violet.

The average Manchester United fan by distance from Old Trafford lives in Toulouse. Similarly, the average Chelsea fan lives in Vladivostok.

'Teen Spirit' is a brand of barbecue lighting fluid.

BBC newsreaders have special operations to make them talk like that.

Hair care products that promise bizarre styling options are usually based on fox semen.

Prototype Daleks could hitch up their skirts and can-can.

The rules of Karma - you get what you give - do not apply when abusing petty minded officials who are trying to deliberately ruin your day.

Henry VIII did not have Anne Boleyn executed. In fact she accidentally cut off her own head while shaving her beard. Henry took the blame to save her family's embarrassment.

The city of Liverpool is in another dimension.

Scientists believe that more than 80% of dinosaurs will never be correctly identified because their bones were made of dried mud and hence didn't so much fossilise as wash away.

Christianity is the product of a spiteful mind, instilling fear and guilt based on the teaching of a God's unconditional love.

Kent is a separate land mass to the rest of the UK and levitates eight inches above the North Sea which stretches beneath he Kentish landmass all the way to Pembury and Tunbridge Wells.

Marmite was originally marketed as an insect repellent.

The World Wrestling Federation 'war cry' of 'Let's get ready to rumble!' was originally 'let's get ready to rumba' until it was realised that most steroid bound knucklehead Americans don't have the grace or rhythm required.

The sequel to 'Hideous Kinky' was to have been titled 'Repugnant Pervert' but the title failed at the test audience stage.

Psychotherapy is a martial art closely resembling ten pin bowling.

Thermos flasks know how to keep hot things hot and cold things cold because there's a little switch on the bottom.

Helen of Troy was noted for her skills in playing Subbuteo.

Original member of the Rolling Stones Brian Jones was murdered because he'd started a collection of moss and lichens.

Sony Corporation started out making gymslips for middle-aged salarymen.

The planet Earth has four suns, but they're always perfectly aligned so you can only see the nearest one.

Acne shows the degree of gullibility in the individual.

Desmond Lynam is a God in Nepal.

The Ramones song '53rd and 3rd' commemorates the street corner on which Dee Dee Ramone ran a newspaper vending booth.

According to the Daily Mail all PlayStation games with an 18 certificate contain subliminal messages urging teenagers to commit mass murder.

Orville the Duck was served shredded in 2003 in a Chinese restaurant in Feltham.

San Antonio in Texas was named by a man who thought he was about to sneeze.

The most popular tribute act in America is called 'Vegans and Roses - a hippy tribute to Axl Rose'.

Because of the flood of D-list celebrities as a result of such TV shows as Big Brother, the Warhol Institute has reviewed its original claim of '15 minutes of fame' to 2.9 seconds.

London Zoo disappeared for a week in 1984, replaced by a large hole in the ground. It was a publicity stunt by Duran Duran, promoting 'The Reflex'. Nick Rhodes thought it up while pissed and their management was too scared to point out it was a stupid idea.

Dr Harold Shipman was a direct descendant of Florence Nightingale, and believed he was tasked with counter-balancing her work tending the unwell and long-term parasitic.

Pork chops are made from sheep meat, hence their other popular name, 'lamb chops'.

Your balance is controlled by an ever-spinning gyroscope in your head. Excessive consumption of alcohol temporarily slows down the rate of spin causing you to stagger around like a drunken fool.

The phrase 'hung like a donkey' dates back to the 16th century when merely being a donkey was irrefutable evidence of witchcraft - a crime which warranted the death penalty.

Consensus among owls is that if they could hover they'd be 100% satisfied with their lot. As it stands they cannot hover and compensate instead with overly twisty necks and huge collections of sci-fi DVDs.

Paedophilia is a mandatory six week course taken by trainee Catholic priests.

Gary Glitter ran a very successful puppy farm prior to his arrest.

Children's television favourite 'Blue Peter' was named as a reference to an incident involving presenter Peter Purves and a big bucket of woad.

The 70s rock band Vanilla Fudge were not named after a confectionery but an inter-racial sexual practice involving anal penetration.

Too many bears kept in a box are liable to spontaneously combust. Too many is generally considered to be six.

Kumquats cannot grow in soil solely fertilised with semen despite their name.

Mr Kendal Mintcake was a runner-up in Mastermind 1975. His specialist subjects were 'confectionary for mountain climbers', 'hiking and the rations required' and '14th century religious genocides'.

A baby's natural first language is Japanese. This will be abandoned for the language of their parents as they grow older and by the age of three they will remember nothing of it. Japanese babies can speak business-level Japanese by the age of two because of their natural advantage.

Every third word that Esther Rantzen speaks is 'cock'.

The world's most prolific recording artist is James Last (with his Orchestra), who records and releases every single 'Swinging Disco Party' he holds; three a week for the last 42 years. James says 'you haven't truly partied until you've heard our Kiss medley with a bossa nova beat!'

Iraq is the only country in the world that has a name beginning with the letter 'I'.

Home brew lager kills more germs than bleach.

Due to a mathematical paradox, the cube root of 27 can either be 3, or 242. This fact can be used to explain the packs of jet-powered badgers that inhabit the Norfolk Broads.

Until the age of 14, Jethro Tull singer and flautist Ian Anderson only had one leg.

Smoking counteracts the effects of radiation poisoning.

Stuffing an ostrich full of sand is the best way to avoid being seen by hungry predators.

Rabbit flavoured ice cream is not available in supermarkets because the rabbit meat prevents the ice cream from freezing until it reaches -120 degrees C, far beyond the capability of most home freezers.

Coal is deep blue, rendering the phrase 'as black as coal' obsolete.

Amphetamines when force fed to rabbits promote cardiac failure which in turn accelerates their evolution to their next natural stage i.e. as something for lunch.

The speed of sound in turpentine is exactly twice the speed of light in a vacuum.

Drunks naturally talk Finnish.

The town of Mansfield is being moved brick by brick to the South of France to avoid an outbreak of SAD.

Most men with grey hair list 'aggravating thigh injuries' in their top ten hobbies.

In Cockney Rhyming Slang, a 'squirrel' is £36.

Jazz musician Dizzy Gillespie had three mouths.

Kidbrooke in south east London is the first place in the western world to achieve an average negative IQ.

In 1972 the Jamaican state broadcasting company paid the BBC over £100,000 for rights to broadcast 'The Herbs' in the belief that it was a series of public information films.

Pubic Quiffs were popular before lice were invented. Some stood out almost four feet from the groin.

Super-bouncy balls, popular with children in the 1970s, were made from rendered down greyhounds that had become too old to race.

Motorways in Ireland by law must have a subterranean leprechaun crossing every three and a half miles.

The double skinned hull of the Titanic was filled with pebbles for insulation.

Gerbils dyed blue are an ideal substitute for those detergent blocks that you drop in your toilet cistern.

Wayne Rooney is a leak from another dimension.

'Little' Stevie Wonder was nine feet tall at birth.

Tracing Elvis Costello's family tree back for four generations reveals that at least three of his ancestors were not human.

Princess Margaret posed nude for Playboy in 1967 but MI5 forcibly suppressed the publication of the images.

Ewan McGregor is the rightful King of Scotland.

Popular comic character Judge Dredd is based on the adventures of members of the Birmingham Special Patrol Group.

Kippers taste better if they're played Rachmaninov while they're being smoked. It relaxes them.

During its career Sean Connery's wig has been nominated for three Oscars, one Golden Globe and a BAFTA, but has only ever been awarded its 50 metres breaststroke certificate.

'Catting' is a pastime similar to 'dogging', but practitioners have to get to rendezvous points by walking along very thin wall-tops or tree branches while torturing a sparrow.

April Showers brings May flowers or at least did until April died in 1975. April's son Geoff Showers now brings bootleg DVDs to May's son Tony and they sit in Tony's flat all night watching badly copied vintage porn and smoking crack.

On Tuesdays, pi=22.

Without exception the cartoons for Leonardo da Vinci's paintings were funnier than the finished product.

Scientists have finally proven that there is nothing at all that isn't improved by the addition of a beer.

Jeff Lynne (of rock band ELO) is the holder of the Worst Frizzy Hair & Aviator Shades Combo Award, and has been since 1977.

Marilyn Manson only did it for the money. His real career ambition was to be a bank clerk but he got side-tracked.

Chrysler experimented with excrement (methane) powered cars but abandoned the idea because of an inability to maintain fuel consistency at the pump.

While the average human body will decompose to the bones inside three years after burial, Michael Jackson's nose is expected to remain intact until the 24th Century.

The scripts for Star Trek: The Next Generation are the basis of an offshoot of the Kabbalah in which Judaist philosophy has Klingon Rules Of Battle overlaid.

The Dunlop Rubber Company explored the possibilities of cheesecake in tyre manufacture and produced several prototypes, all of which were endorsed by Ayrton Senna.

Steam locomotives are powered by shovelling hamsters into a very small black hole in the firebox.

The composer Handel had no hands and played piano instead with his feet and a complex array of sticks and wires attached to his head. To watch him perform was akin to watching a 'punk rocker' of the 1970s 'spazzing out' 230 years ahead of his time.

Flying under London Bridge upside down in Concorde then performing a loop the loop manoeuvre while playing Microsoft Flight Simulator 2000 will fire up an 'Easter egg' which brings up a simple spreadsheet on the page, allowing you to easily manage your household accounts.

Alternate realities are actually in perpendicular dimensions rather than parallel ones. This explains why you never end up in one when overtaking on motorways.

The perfect drink to accompany roast lamb is axle grease.

Banging two pieces of parmesan cheese together will cause earthquakes in Rome.

David Hasselhoff is the Son Of God.

Anthony Wedgwood Benn invented Royal Doulton's line of kitsch figurines beloved of the old and excessively wealthy.

'Jumping Jehosophat!' of popular exclamation fame was fully titled Winston Jehosophat, and was a compulsive masturbator. 'Wanking Winston!' was not however considered to be as acceptable a phrase in polite society.

Rover cars were so named because they were powered by hundreds of tiny dogs running on a conveyor belt under the bonnet.

It is a myth that King Edward I of England was known as the 'Hammer of the Scots'. He actually preferred to be referred to as the 'Fretsaw of the Welsh'.

Were you to mark the position of every telephone exchange in England on a map you would notice that their positions form a giant pentagram.

The late Richard Whitely tiled his kitchen floor with Scrabble® letters.

Actors in the Hollywood Top 100 are bulletproof. Try it! They can't be shot!

Kendal Mint Cake is made in Belgium, is flavoured with chrysanthemums and is strictly speaking a yoghurt, and yet has never been brought to task by the Advertising Standards Authority.

Chaka Khan was the King of the Mongols.

Pigeons are hollow and explode like a bag of crisps if you stamp on them.

Bigfoot takes size 28 (EUR) shoes. He has to order them especially from select branches of Marks and Spencer.

Time is not (as many philosophers have stated) an illusion. Time is an oily secretion put out by seabirds from glands near their anuses.

In 2006 the law was changed to allow doctors to put down the elderly if they have terminal illnesses or are just too damn tedious to live.

Chuck Berry's 'Duck Walk' was invented when he tried to stamp on a mallard with his right foot while his left was nailed to a piece of wood. The bird lived but a rock legend was born.

In 1953 Manchester United had a goalkeeper called Perry Stalsis. In 1992 The Guinness Book of World Records finally recognised this as the funniest footballer name ever.

The heart of the Internet is in London but its groin is in San Francisco.

80s pop sensations 'Adam and The Ants' were forced to disband after a lawsuit brought by Kettering Trading Standards Authority accused the band of not actually being insects. This followed a previous unsuccessful action in 1968 against ? and the Mysterians.

The vast majority of children's TV is scripted by especially hired people with severe learning difficulties in the mistaken belief that children are morons too.

Weblogging (also known as 'blogging) has been declared the single biggest cause of cancer in the under 50s by the General Medical Council.

Smoking more than 80 cigarettes a day can improve eyesight, virility and ability to knit. Results are not guaranteed however.

Chicago, 'The Windy City', got its nickname after vegetarianism was invented there in 1914.

Prince Charles has bright red cheeks because he's just started teething.

Wearing black nail varnish is punishable by death should the crime take place outside the London Borough of Camden.

If you vigorously shake the pages of the Daily Mail the words will jumble themselves up into an order which frequently makes more sense than the original. This phenomenon means that it is advisable to buy your copy at a newsagent at the end of a very bumpy road.

Coca-Cola is known for formerly containing cocaine but other brands have similar dark histories - a half pint of original formulation Cresta cherryade contained enough amphetamine to keep a child awake for three days, while Kia Ora was a cover for a cat's urine smuggling operation - cat's urine, when ingested, having similar effects to LSD but with terrifying 'waking nightmare' side effects, hence the phrase 'I'm not drinking that's cat's piss'. It was a popular 'drink spike' used by the CIA, Mossad and MI5 in the 1970s until an antidote was discovered and similarly retailed as 'Panda Pops' (mandarin flavour).

Princess Diana was strangely drawn to drummers in black metal bands. It's believed she was pen friends with Abaddon from Venom.

Simon Cowell has an oil painting of himself as an old man dated 1872 in his attic.

Dead Daily Mail columnist Linda Lee Potter was the mother of teenage wizard Harry Potter.

2-Tone Records had their corporate colours as black and white not through any racial harmony statement but because their printer ran out of green ink.

Coca-Cola is well known for its spermicidal properties but it's less well known that 7-Up is the ideal enema solution.

Miles Davis achieved his unique sound by filling his trumpet with radishes.

Anteaters do not in fact eat ants. They eschew all forms of insect in favour of cream buns and gunpowder.

After the Bush election victory of 2004 there was an 81% drop-off in the purchase of coast-to-coast US flights that stop off halfway across for fear of attack on the big silver bird by inbred halfwit locals.

Watching westerns on a flat screen TV will increase the frequency of maintenance visits by your local technology specialists, as the drain is much narrower than on an old CRT set and is therefore more likely to get clogged up with dead cowboys. It is however possible to clean the drain yourself by pouring 'Mr Muscle Drain Unblocker' over the main circuit board and leaving overnight.

Kittens are more volatile than firelighters.

The average 15 year old will attempt to smoke 80% of the spices in their mother's spice rack in a vain attempt to get high. Ironically, the only 'buzz' available from a spice rack is by scraping off the varnish on the rack itself and smoking that instead. Clearly this does not apply to natural wood finishes.

The camera was invented in Greece, near Mount Olympus.

If the digits in your phone number can be mathematically manipulated to reach the number 27 you can claim a one-off prize of ten thousand pounds from the Premium Bonds.

The standard railway track gauge in Luxembourg is nine miles.

In space, candles accumulate wax from the atmosphere when they burn.

Rolls-Royce jet engines are actually big cages containing flocks of giant moths.

Chelsea Clinton won 'Best Mongrel' at Crufts 2002.

Chickens can be trained to fetch the paper from the front door like a dog but it takes more than three dozen to deal with a copy of the Observer (replete with pull-out sections etc.)

Cuddles the Monkey in his post Keith Harris downward spiral ekes out a living working as a rent boy specialising in bestial practises.

8% of the public are hermaphrodite. Generally they pretend to be one or the other but live their lives eternally single and always go to the toilet sitting down in a cubicle. They die lonely and afraid.

Brett Anderson, ex-lead singer with Suede, still brushes himself down with a soft brush every morning before he leaves the house to spend his giro.

Oasis is Blur putting on Mancunian accents and performing as a Beatles tribute act.

The paper fragments found in the bottom of high-volume office laser printers when mixed with water make an excellent substitute for mayonnaise.

Prior to post-natal surgery a dog is actually your eight-legged friend, given that they are closely related to spiders.

When Hannibal crossed the Alps with elephants in order to attack Rome he hadn't reckoned on the Romans releasing hundreds of white mice into battle, rendering the elephants ineffective as a fighting force.

Apple's popular personal music player the 'iPod' was originally designed as a storage unit for genetically modified peas.

Adding more than eight cloves of garlic to any dish will result in your house sinking into the North Sea.

Not only do some people see sounds as colour but a small subset of these people see colours as musical notes written out on a stave, usually in F major.

The M4 follows a ley line from Swindon to J7, Slough West. This is why it smells of excrement immediately after that junction, and is nothing at all to do with the huge sewage plant next to the motorway.

Magazines aimed at film buffs such as 'Empire' have their pages impregnated with Mandrax.

Leonardo da Vinci invented the Fast Breeder Reactor but never built one as he didn't know what Uranium or Plutonium were.

According to a recent article in the Guardian you can now buy grandchildren on Amazon.co.uk.

Gott le of gear

Adolf Hitler was a glove puppet operated by Josef Goebbels.

Marmite makes an effective spermicide. It should be smeared liberally on both partners' relevant surfaces.

If you see the words 'I wish my girlfriend was this dirty' inscribed in grime on the back of a white transit van, you are not looking at a hilarious joke perpetrated by a halfwit · rather it is a Masonic sign directing local lodge members to the nearest off license.

Every song on the first two Duran Duran albums had the subliminal message 'give us your money' embedded in each track.

Old chocolate goes white when all the sugar is converted to alcohol.

'Pale Ale' is produced by sucking all the goodness from a pint of dark mild.

In 1967 Rolf Harris gave birth to a dingo.

The Tiger Moth biplane was originally made from real tiger skins and moth wings.

In an Orwellian twist Davina McColl while hosting the next series of Big Brother will be forced to declare there are five people still in the house regardless of the number actually remaining.

A bowlful of mucus charged with 33,000 volts for a split second will produce sentient life-forms.

Roof tiles were invented in 1978 and were retro-fitted to all houses in the UK less than 130 years old. A campaign of disinformation followed to convince the populace that they had been around for centuries.

A standard issue NHS colostomy bag has the added benefit of keeping tomato soup warm for up to eight hours.

Classic Syd Barrett album 'The Madcap Laughs' is a musical biography of Adolf Schmitzer, insane comedy hat maker to the stars.

After their brief pop star career of the late 1960s 'The 1910 Fruitgum Company' changed their name to Glaxo and went into the Dangerous Chemicals business.

Thanks to new EU laws British trawler men will shortly be limited to shooting fish in a barrel. They will be required to supply their own barrel and fish, as well as being restricted to using an air rifle.

Abba's 'Arrival' album is simply Pink Floyd's 'Dark Side Of The Moon' album played backwards at 45rpm.

In 2001 Leonid Brezhnev was placed #163 in a Top Comedians of All Time poll, three places higher than Jim Davidson and fourteen spots above Jimmy Cricket.

Magazines for pigeon fanciers may not be sold to minors.

Tony Blair is really comedian Eddie Izzard wearing a Tony Blair mask.

Everton Football Club's original nickname was 'The Dog Toffeemen'.

Bernard Matthews has begun marketing tabby cats as a cheap alternative to the traditional Christmas roast turkey. You can buy them in any branch of Lidl, William Low or Netto.

As well as osprey and rock badger, the book of Leviticus also specifically outlaws the eating of tapir, plain chocolate, and cheese and onion crisps.

Osama Bin Laden was a turkey in very heavy and convincing makeup. His hatred of the West was rooted in the West's habit of roasting his feathered comrades as a means of celebrating Christmas.

Jimi Hendrix was a dirigible in disguise.

Sod's Law was first postulated by William Sod, a bricklayer to the court of King Henry IV.

Between them, the members of Welsh rock band Budgie know all the secrets of the universe.

'Road accidents' are nothing of the sort. They're all deliberate acts of sabotage.

The most popular operation carried out in the private medical suites deep in the bowels of the Houses Of Parliament is the operation to remove one's moral beliefs, in which a small piece of brain is excised and replaced with an equal amount of canine faeces, enabling the politician to think like and share the beliefs and moral structures of a City trader.

When looking at a symphony orchestra onstage you will find the cream horns just to the right of the cream oboes, and in front of the cream tympani.

Results of a survey conducted on the internet has shown that while 85% of children own a private jet, only four per cent use it to get to school.

Pork pies are the #1 meditational focus for Zen Buddhists.

There is a section of the Dartford Tunnel that is three weeks in the future, where one can hear the radio from three weeks hence and thus pick up some racing tips. The stretch is only twenty five yards long, and is covered in two seconds at 40mph so most drivers never notice and put it down to poor reception but those in the know stand on the service gantry with an FM radio and an oxygen cylinder.

Fish beer made with hops, water and live herring is highly prized in Norway and costs more than champagne for the best brews.

Six out of ten otters play a mean speed metal bass guitar.

The working title of 'Mein Kampf' was 'Peter and Jane Go To Nuremburg'.

Camden contains the Fourth Gate of Hell - the gate that captures time and joy - which explains the propensity of the locals to dress in the gothic manner, as was fashionable some three decades ago in 1985.

In the 1984 UK General Election the residents of the Bedford North constituency mistakenly voted in a cheese sandwich as their MP with a majority of fourteen thousand.

Gaffa tape is made from cured tapir skins. Similarly all the buildings in Cowdenbeath Scotland, are built using bricks made from compressed cow.

Cats float better if you tie a brick to their collar.

The song lyric 'New York New York, so good they named it twice' is untrue. For absolute accuracy, the lyric should be 'New York New York, they named it twice because most Americans are incapable of grasping the meaning of a two word phrase the first time they hear it, and hence require repetition'. But that didn't scan.

The Lunar Rover that traversed the surface of the moon was based on the chassis of an Austin Maestro with the engine from a Suffolk Punch lawnmower and the brown vinyl seats from a Mk 3 Ford Cortina. It was built in a scrapyard near Mold in North Wales.

In any collision the coefficient of restitution (or 'bounciness') is a randomly generated number.

The estate of the late George Best has donated his liver to medical science fiction.

Cheddar cheese becomes Emmental when holes are drilled into it. Nothing less than a 3/4' bit though.

There are fourteen million types of spider, all identical.

Paul McCartney donated all royalties from his hit single 'The Frog Chorus' to the Royal Society For The Promotion of Hitting Frogs With Shovels.

Britney Spears has a sister called Asparagus.

Maxwell House brand coffee granules are desiccated parts of the rotting corpse of Robert Maxwell.

MILK or CREAM?

'Lord Kitchener' was actually a nickname for Lord Ffanshawe of Trewethicke. He was so called because he found debates in the House of Lords immensely dull and was usually found in the kitchen making tea for the others. After three years he knew who wanted tea or coffee, black or white, with or without sugar.

If you have poor eyesight you can still pass your driving test by convincing the tester that you have extra-sensory perception.

Only 47 people in the UK spoke the Queen's English throughout the 1950s, and they were all employed as announcers for the BBC, for both radio and television services. A good fake posh accent could net upwards of £300 per week in 1952, equivalent in today's money to the wages of the entire Arsenal squad including the reserves.

Pope Septius VII was the seventh son of a seventh son and had magical powers but was so massively inbred his IQ was just 61 and thus was not smart enough to learn how to unleash them.

Pope Septius VI was the son of a pig farmer and smelt like curdled shit.

Archaeologists have finally worked out the rules to Elgin marbles.

All members of the band 'The Lemonheads' actually had heads made from citrus fruit.

34% of Channel 5 output is cross-talk from other channels.

Amphetamines were invented for the Royal Family to sprinkle on their breakfast cereal.

A human mother's milk if bottled and left at room temperature for 24 hours will naturally become Yakult yoghurt, and that's how they make it.

84% of Dr Who fans have difficulty talking to girls, mainly because they don't fancy them.

Lesbians repel chocolate sandwich spread. If applied to a lesbian it hovers 3/8 of an inch above the skin. Honey is actively attracted however and the average lesbian can absorb a 454g jar of honey in less than three hours under lab conditions.

You can increase the size of your brain by dressing as a giant chicken and bothering goats.

All the members of second rate heavy metal band 'The Rods' could only see in monochrome as they had no cones in their eyes.

Davy Jones, ex of the Monkees, is really named David Bowie. David Bowie's real name is Nils Lofgren and Nils Lofgren's real name is Bonnie Langford.

Authentic Scotch Eggs should be marinated in vats of whisky no less than eight years old for at least a week before serving.

Boscastle was a Centre of Gym Excellence until the green mats and the horse got washed away.

Spermicide was originally the act of ending one's life by deliberately drowning in a barrel of semen.

It is possible to see the Eiffel Tower from the top of Blackpool Tower. Curiously, this effect does not work in reverse.

'Singin' In The Rain' was originally a six hour diatribe against the slave industry until it was substantially rewritten. Gene Kelly was to have played a cotton plantation owner with a wooden leg.

Steven Hawking and George W Bush went to the same school. In their final examinations, George sneakily swapped the papers, thus reversing the decisions the Gods made for the men. The halfwit should have been laid waste by a muscle disease and the genius should have become President of the USA.

A sub-clause in the Smuggling Act of 1756 makes it illegal for anyone to breathe more than five times a minute. This is why lovemaking was so languid in the late eighteenth century; to get overly excited was to court a death sentence.

Star Trek's Klingons were originally called Winnits by Gene Rodenberry, the show's creator.

The Romans were so called because of their tendency to wander about the place.

In 2003 British law courts ruled that there is nothing sadder, pathetic and deluded than a middle aged menopausal woman who believes she's a better singer than Barbara Streisand.

Chalk is an isotope of cheese.

'My Little Pony's come to life after midnight and roam the countryside in packs, terrorising feral cats.

Bernard Manning and Bernard Matthews were the same person. It took Bernard Matthews six hours to put on his 'repugnant' makeup to effect the transformation.

Ex-punk-lite singer Hazel O'Connor wrote the theme tune to every television show broadcast on the 9th of January, 2003.

Audi TT cars are grown in vats of primordial ooze before being sold to dickheads.

Jackie Stallone's hairdresser receives a danger money payment for every appointment.

The Prince of Darkness requires the sacrifice of one kitten or puppy for every domestic property connected to broadband internet. The pile of pet corpses is just outside Rainham in Kent.

John Smith, the former Labour party leader, was assassinated by the Vatican's secret forces.

Newspaper colour supplements make better bedding for hamsters than the regular monochrome pages.

Imelda Marcos is 163 years old and is kept alive by regular injections of suede water repellent; the huge collection of shoes is merely a cover for bulk water repellent purchases at Shoe World in Droitwich.

God loves to suck on a Fisherman's Friend.

Bile is an acceptable substitute for Marmite.

Grave robbing is legally acceptable if the deceased owed the robber more than a fiver.

Cricket bats are actually made from lots of small grasshoppers, compressed in a machine which provides a pressure of thirty tons per square inch.

No-one who is actually intelligent believes in 'intelligent design'.

The national sport of Egypt is complaining loudly about sand.

The musical 'Grease' was John Travolta's first attempt at making a biopic of L. Ron Hubbard.

Due to an unfortunate mix up during a failed application to join the EU in 1996, the capital of Chile is now Mansfield.

Meat chutneys are very popular in Brazil; rabbit, wildebeest and penguin are particular favourites despite the letter two not being native.

The hydraulic systems on Ford motor cars were initially powered by the high blood pressure of a very short, fat Texan man imprisoned under the bonnet.

Cast iron saucepans are deemed unholy by the Vatican.

Popular 'heavy metal' magazine 'Kerrang!' is printed on skin flayed from virgins' backs with blood donated weekly by Ozzy Osbourne, self-styled 'Prince of Darkness'. This explains why each copy smells faintly of pork.

Fish worship was made mandatory in Omaha in 1893. It was outlawed in 1901, reinstated in 1904 and finally carved in stone in 1911. The stone was used for sacrificial fish disembowelling until 1924, when it was outlawed as a by-product of the prohibition laws which were never actually repealed, just mislaid.

The premise for the TV show Space 1999 is a true story but it was covered up by the CIA. There has been a Moon base since 1985 and the moon was blown out of orbit in 1999, when it was replaced by a large beach ball filled with helium on an 800m piece of fishing line. This is why you can no longer see the moon from the window of an aircraft while it's in flight.

'Slacker' rock star Beck was so named because he was born in a trout river in Northumberland.

Traffic cones are acceptable currency in most student union bars.

Since 1973 newly employed Radio 1 disc jockeys have traditionally been the offspring of a goat and a wet cardboard box.

Popular aliens 'The Greys' actually do exist and a family of eight of them was captured by the French government in 1997. An insider who spoke to The Guardian newspaper in 1999 said 'They all look and sound a bit like Jeremy Clarkson'.

Cheap American toffee sweets 'Tootsie Rolls' were originally made from human toes, covered in chocolate.

Walt Disney's assertion that 'all our dreams can come true if we have the courage to pursue them' was adequately disproved by Hitler.

The steel mesh around the top of the Monument in the City Of London was put there in the eighteenth century to prevent inquisitive cattle falling off, having wandered up in search of foodstuffs or similar.

Charisma is a quality that many infants accidentally throw up when they're babes in arms, leaving them to become sullen teens and later, full blown delinquents.

Alcohol cures all known ills without exception.

Noel Edmonds started out in the music business as a roadie for the Krankies. He looked after Wee Jimmy Krankie's phenomenal cocaine demands.

Less than 1% of pro-life advocates choose to adopt the children they so want to see born into families that do not want and/or cannot support them. Rather, they herd them into abandoned football arenas where they are reared for food.

Excessive ingestion of radishes can cause delusions of grandeur in rabbits.

Hercule Poirot was a real person. It was Agatha Christie who didn't really exist.

Australia is an optical illusion caused by light refracting through sheep living in New Zealand.

In Uzbekistan one can 'buy' a mayoral election for eight hundredweight of fresh vegetables (assorted).

It gets so muddy in Waitrose car parks that it's essential to own a four wheel drive vehicle for use when you go shopping.

Senator Joe McCarthy, noted for his anti-communist witch-hunts in the 60s, was eventually hung by his own tabard when he deigned that the name Joe (as in Stalin) was an inherently communist name. He was stoned to death by rednecks within twenty-four hours of his proclamation in 1967.

In the First World War, the combatants changed ends every 45 minutes with 10 minutes out for orange halves and a pep talk from the captain.

SAS 'hero' Andy McNabb's first 'novel based on a true story' had the working title of 'I Shat Myself and Ran Away'.

The British Royal Family's original surname was not Von Klinkerhoffen as is often espoused; rather it was Jacob-Kreutzfeld. The name is also used for the human form of BSE since the first sufferer was a Royal - the Queen Mother, who contracted it in 1967.

In 1978 the Land Speed Record was taken by a Morris Marina 1300 but it was disqualified on grounds of credibility.

Shredded Wheat were originally going to be called Strawberry Flavoured Anal Intruders until someone pointed out that that a 100% wheat breakfast cereal with no added sugar, salt or artificial additives is in fact none of those things.

There were originally eighteen wonders of the Ancient World including the Compost Heap at Sparta, the Temple of Bernard, The Statue of Sid James and the Cuboids of Sheffield.

During the Second World War rodents were farmed for their meat. Rats were force fed grain to produce something akin to pate de fois gras.

The members of Swedish pop sensations Abba took their names from phrases in Dylan Thomas' 'Under Milk Wood'.

35% of women having IVF treatment are given pig semen instead of human. The doctors know it won't give any sort of result but it makes them laugh in the pub after work, and the high failure rate keeps 'em coming back for more, spending thousands every time. Porsches don't pay for themselves after all.

The Who, The Jam and The Kinks all started out under the name 'Streptococcal Balalaika', a fashionable type of LSD in the 60s.

'A little bit of what you fancy does you no harm' is a popular phrase among adulterers but less so among gun barrel licking fetishists of whose numbers several dozen are killed yearly in gun masturbatory fantasies gone horribly wrong.

Clothes horses were originally made of horse bones, the thighs and spine being especially useful for hanging blankets over. The very rich would have an entire horse skeleton reconstructed to hang clothes on the dry. The modern steel (and/or plastic) alternative became popular when people started washing and bathing daily and society noticed that the wealthy smelled like equine death.

Because the South African unit of currency is the Rand, a rich man in Johannesburg is said to be Randy. Conversely, a rich man in

Vietnam where the currency is the Dong is not 'Dongy'; rather, he is 'hung like a horse'.

Marmalade was originally created by accident in a Nazi germ warfare laboratory.

The crusty baguette is a giant version of the cricket, killed, dried, de-winged and de-legged and baked for 30 minutes at gas mark 6.

'Jif' cleansing liquid changed its name to 'Cif' because 'Chlamydia' was a silly name for a household cleaner.

Angel Delight is so named because in 1956 it was the #1 favourite dessert among celestial beings. The last survey (in 2002) put it at #94, with McFlurries (all varieties) at #93. Rollmop herring was at #92.

Ariel Sharon's sons are named Persil, Bold and Dreft, and - in a break with tradition - the female twins are named Domestos and Parozone.

Jeff Lynne of ELO owns the patent rights to all types of hair salon curling tongs and 'Aviator' style sunglasses; hence his ceaseless promotion of both items.

Augustus Caesar's hobby was pulling the wings off bees.

Viagra was invented to repel greenfly from runner beans.

Despite what you see in the movie, Anne Widdicombe is really Spartacus.

'The Incredible Hulk' comic is in fact Marvel boss Stan Lee's autobiography which he serialised and self-published.

Eleanor Rigby was a brand of deodorant in the 1960s, as was Leader of the Gang in the '70s and Planet Earth in the '80s. All three tracks had a significant influence on a young Kurt Cobain.

O'Reilly (the computer book publisher)'s biggest selling title ever is 'JavaBeans for Stalinists'.

92% of health and safety courses are held in rooms with no ventilation and exposed live wires beneath the metal chairs - thus being neither healthy nor safe.

Bella Emberg had such a density that cream buns would be trapped in orbit around her.

Should an American Presidential election end in a draw, the winner is decided by a 'best of three' game of Stone-Paper-Scissors.

Hairdressing salons which have names that include a bad pun ('Curl up and Dye', 'Hair Today') will be made illegal by 2019, and their owners impaled on spikes.

Cheap sausages have been identified as the primary cause of the vast majority of domestic disputes.

93% of accountants were bullied at school.

In Norway, it is illegal to refer to a mobile 'phone as 'a mobile phone', as strictly speaking, they are not mobile. They must always be referred to as 'portable 'phones'.

Leonard Nimoy is allergic to William Shatner. This is why they never touched in Star Trek or indeed real life.

Princess Diana was a hermaphrodite.

The character of Gail Tilsley in Coronation Street was originally to have been played by Elizabeth Taylor who had signed the contract with Granada while drunk. It was by similar means that Judy Garland was signed up for (but never appeared in) The Likely Lads.

Studies have proven that 93% of members of student political societies are ugly and need somewhere to vent their sexual energy, even if it's in a non-sexual way. The remaining 7% are there for a bet, usually £100 to the man who sleeps with the ugliest bushpig available. Places like the Socialist Worker Student Society provide rich pickings.

One packet of Walker's Roast Chicken flavour crisps contains 160% of the RDA of roast chicken flavouring. Too little roast chicken flavouring can cause sprouting of feathers, scratching in the dust and involuntary clucking.

Einstein developed his Theory of Relativity while working as a lifeguard at Chertsey Swimming Pool and watching the breasts of nubile teen girls beneath sheer swimsuits.

David Bowie's different coloured eyes are a result of being held face down in a vat of acid as a child. This also explains his whiney voice.

Most of the world's great religious texts were originally published by Mills and Boon.

Researchers for Channel 4's Richard and Judy show have discovered a man in Leicester who has grown a marrow in the shape of Esther Rantzen.

Laws in Eire are written as Limericks.

87% of company fire alarm/building evacuation incidents are caused by the inappropriate use of kitchen equipment for sexual gratification.

Early genetic experiments to give a pig the IQ of a low grade human resulted in Jade Goody.

Because custard powder is explosive, you can add it to warm water to make a cheap, effective and pleasant smelling alternative to 4 star petrol.

It is possible to get your local telephone supplier to reduce the amount you pay by 50% by simply writing the words 'dogs and fish and salad rolls' on the bill in crayon and posting it to the Chancellor of the Exchequer.

There has never yet been an advertising campaign encouraging the ignorant and pointless to kill themselves because every advertising exec to have worked on such an account has ended their own life within a fortnight of accepting the contract.

The appeasement of the Suez Crisis of 1956 was due to everyone wanting to go home.

Sunblock can also be used to block streets, prolapses and (perversely) unblock noses, when deployed in sufficient quantity.

Dennis the Menace was based on the real-life childhood experiences of Dennis Taylor, the famous snooker player. Beryl The Peril is based on that of Beryl Reid. They both grew up in Trowbridge.

A catalytic converter on your car is made up of a cat with an exhaust pipe rammed into its mouth, forcing its bodily organs to absorb the toxic elements put out by the car.

The 70's sci-fi TV show 'Sapphire and Steel' was originally going to be an update of 'Arsenic and Old Lace'.

Cryogenics started out as the science of preserving people in vats of tears before the tears were frozen and a state of near-stasis was achieved.

The last original song was recorded in 1972 by Donny Osmond. Since then every song that has been written has sounded vaguely like something that went before even if the songwriter was unaware because all the available tune permutations have been used up.

Electric whisks can cause enough ripples in gravity to unbalance a mouse at a range of three metres.

The concept of Chinese Whispers is well noted as the mis-repetition of a phrase because it was partially inaudible when heard. A similar effect occurs in clubs and bars where the music is moronic 4/4 house music at 113dB and even shouting isn't enough to be understood. It's known as the Harlow Bellow, and those familiar with it carry a trainspotter style pad on which to write out their conversations.

Egg mayonnaise was originally created as a way of using eggs that had gone off by hard boiling them and then shredding and mixing with vinegar and cat vomit to disguise the 'rotten egg' taste. Contrary to expectation, a mixture of vinegar, cat vomit and rotten eggs smells and tastes like fresh hard boiled eggs in mayonnaise. In the 1920s the recipe was changed to that known and loved today, simply because it didn't involve getting scratched to pieces by a cat that didn't want to throw up.

Crème brûlée is a bowl full of bull semen that's been assaulted with a blowtorch and had Demerara sprinkled on top. In Spain it was traditionally served as the dessert after a meal of fried bulls' testicles, the famous Spanish dish.

Victorian 'Penny Dreadful' comics actually cost three pounds and weren't all that bad.

Wheelchair-bound super scientist Stephen Hawking is hoping to take part in beach volleyball at the London Olympics.

Elton John was once admitted to hospital with a dead man's head lodged in his rectum. He told staff it got there while he was vacuuming in the nude.

The Humber Bridge is made from compressed copies of the Daily Express.

Belgium has the highest rate of fat languid frogs per capita in the world.

Head lice breed inside your skull and creep out through your ears and nose during the night.

The average two year old child can pull a fridge/freezer three feet before collapsing from exhaustion. This figure is less if his parents do not stand over him brandishing a whip and bellowing 'we're all moving house together, you will do your share'.

Groups of white mice can, in times of extreme danger, bond together to form a single gestalt rodent entity which measures over twenty feet long, walks on its back legs and can clear buildings of up to eight storeys in a single bound.

The term 'jobbing musician' came about in the 19th century when out of work drummers and pipers were employed by debt collection agencies to beat up old ladies who had fallen behind with their outrageously high interest payments.

Fish giblets when worn as a wig can cure baldness.

German politicians are awarded three years' extra time in office if they share a surname with a Peanuts character; hence the lengthy service of Gerhard Schroeder, even though he changed his name to Schroeder by deed poll. Wilhelm von Pigpen was excluded from the German Parliament because 'Pigpen' was only a nickname.

Washing your hair in urine will increase your chance of playing cricket for England by 14%.

Anyone who can walk five miles without having to have a sit down and a rest is eligible for membership of the Order of the Garter.

Drivel is a negotiable currency.

Jesus never rode a bike. He actually drove a Ferrari; hence the more accurate exclamation 'Christ in a penis extension!'

The Reverend Myung Moon was born in Burnley and was christened David Michael Flaherty by his Irish parents. His Asian appearance is the result of £35,000-worth of plastic surgery, skin grafts and vocal coaching.

George W Bush's nicknames are 'Dubya' and 'Shrub', but at school he was known as 'Dorkboy' and 'That Twat Bush'.

Jesus originally had twenty-two disciples, but had the extra ones quietly drowned when he realised they'd make paintings of the Last Supper look too crowded.

On 28th June, 1978, Mr James Henderson of Melton Mowbray counted 3,146,229 sheep, before falling asleep - a world record. He started counting in 1971 and it took 34,000 cups of coffee to keep him going to the world record.

Shakespearian tragedy 'King Lear' was based on the life of limerick writer and artist Edward Lear.

The Sun is only 2 million miles outside the Earth's atmosphere, eight times as far away as the moon. It's twelve miles across and is expected to go supernova by the year 2053, at which point the Earth will go cold and woolly mammoths will again roam the planet.

Apples are nude oranges.

1960s dance crazes 'The Mashed Potato', 'The Watoosie' and 'The HitchHike' were invented by the KGB to promote socialist and communist ideologies in the United States.

George W Bush is 98% simian and 2% crab.

The CIA is working on 'stupid drugs' to keep the populace of America pacified once they become immune to the effects of Reality TV. The British Government is watching with interest.

Llamas can appear to be in more than one place at once due to their ability to travel at light speed.

Pigeons are descended from pigs.

84% of business meetings give no positive result at all; indeed, 67% of meetings with durations of more than 60 minutes give rise to deep vein thrombosis.

An email will get to its destination quicker if it has an image of a first class stamp as an attachment.

Bicycles on which the freewheel has been disabled such as those favoured by hipsters can reverse time if ridden backwards at 13.4mph. For reasons as yet unexplained this does not work within the E8 postcode of London where many such hipsters reside.

'Strange' quarks are so called because if you try and engage them in conversation they look just over your shoulder and mutter about conspiracies.

88% of washed up pop stars commit suicide within three years of their last Top 40 place.

James Herriot was the pseudonym adopted by James Alfred Wight for his popular vet books. It is little known that James Herriot was also the name of a Yorkshire animal sex pervert and abattoir worker of the same era and who would have interfered with several of Mr Wight's patients.

A white paper based on the premise of 'Logan's Run' - that people should be put to sleep at a certain age; in the film 35, in the legal proposal 60 - was accepted by the House of Commons but rejected by the House of Lords in 2002.

Substituting a child's brain with toffee at birth will make him or her more likely to graduate with honours on any BA degree course from any British 'redbrick' university.

A good cry makes you feel better because it leaches the toxins from your brain. That's why your cheeks appear dirty from the tears afterwards.

Dog food manufacturers smell of mint when shot in the knees with any weapon of a calibre greater than .45. Smaller bore weapons will make them smell of Earl Grey tea. The reason is believed to be hormonal.

Richie Edwards, disappearing guitarist with the Manic Street Preachers is in fact not dead. He moved to America, had extensive plastic surgery, lost his Welsh accent through speech therapy and changed his name to Britney Spears, whereupon he got a job presenting the Mickey Mouse Club.

The phrase 'thick as pigshit' comes from the time when pig faeces were dried and formed into bricks for constructing peasant housing. A pigshit brick had six times the density of a normal house brick, repelled mosquitos and acted as a gravity sink, drawing any levitating cream buns into orbit - a boon for the starving peasant. They became outmoded during the cholera epidemic of 1724, when society scientist Sir William Hobbyhorse realised the cream in the buns was the cholera carrier, and forced an Act through Parliament to make the burning of all pigshit bricks mandatory under punishment of arrest for culpable homicide; the ensuing chaos as landlords torched their residents' pigshit brick houses left tens of thousands dead as the burning pigshit bricks multiplied their gravitational coefficients (the heat multiplying the effect) and sucked the residents back into their fiery abodes to their deaths. No landlords were charged in consequence, but Sir Hobbyhorse was himself imprisoned in a pigshit brick prison especially built to be set alight once the prisoner was incarcerated. Sir Hobbyhorse was held in place only by slim ropes which swiftly burned though; of course, he couldn't escape the gravity sink being perpetually dragged back and perished in the flames.

Vodka is distilled from old coffee grounds and goat hair.

The greatest height achieved by a live penguin being shot out of a ground based cannon is 15,400 feet.

The Limpopo River is fictional, invented purely to amuse schoolchildren.

Gaps in walls, or 'windows' were invented in the 11th century and were heavily promoted by the then nascent glass industry.

Smiling for photographs to be used for record covers is considered to be a sin in Germany which is why German death metal album sleeves look like they were recorded by the Osmonds.

There are only three people in the world who know what 'Be-bop-a-lula', 'A-wop-bop-a-loo-bop-a-wop-bam-boom' and 'Shooby-doobee-doo' mean, and they've all been sworn to secrecy by the CIA.

Ben Elton's next West End theatre venture is due to be a big budget stage show based on the music of punk rock types the Anti-Nowhere League and is expected to open in October 2021.

German people can communicate with Austrians by means of their built in Firewire port.

Silk garments can be easily turned into nylon ones by placing them in front of a gas fire for three hours.

Even the dirtiest child can be made spick and span with just ninety seconds in a sandblasting cabinet.

In 2004 John Entwhistle was posthumously awarded a 'Best Way to Die, Ever!' statuette.

Originally the root of all evil was the love of honey.

Putting a white sticker with a green letter P in the back window of your car absolves you of all legal responsibilities when it comes to driving.

Ceremonies held by Freemasons usually involve the swallowing of a handful of angry wasps.

Bob Dylan's 'Blood on the Tracks' LP is a concept album about travelling on London Underground.

Denizens of the eleventh dimension have applied for planning permission for a loft conversion.

Molasses is made of liquefied mole arses, hence the name.

Possession of a 'loyalty card' for any of the major British supermarket chains is enough to get you a job with MI5.

In much the same way that academics tell jokes about the mental inadequacy of people studying media studies, media studies students tell similar jokes about tetraplegics.

Popular Portuguese football team Sporting Lisbon was originally a goldfish fanciers club.

Mars Bars are a good source of energy not because of the glucose they contain but because of the quarter gram of strontium-90 each standard bar contains which raises heart rate and respiration as well as triggering several major cancers.

Anchovies contain a tiny bit of Satan, every one of them.

When questioned, eight out of ten leopards prefer stripes to spots.

The Eiffel Tower is only seven feet high and made of cheese.

Advertising junkie Linda Barker is distantly related to Satan.

Human flesh tastes more like dog than chicken.

'Altoids' are sheep's teeth impregnated with peppermint oil.

The Daily Telegraph was launched in the early 20th century as a fanzine.

'Living in Sin' is less common than you might think. Sin is a village outside Kings Lynn, and has only a population of around 1200.

The inverse relationship between the competence of a company's personnel and its success is finite; every company with inept machinations goes under sooner or later.

119

Wee Jimmy Krankie auditioned for the role of Dr Who. He failed because he couldn't reach the big lever on the Tardis' console.

Staring at your shoes is a good way of telling the time if you haven't got a watch on and it's dark.

Beethoven wrote his first five symphonies in reverse numerical order.

The House of Lords was built from prefab elements in 1854. Its history was falsified shortly after to give it gravitas.

Scientists have stated that if Cher and Michael Jackson were to have produced children, their offspring would have been made of Lego.

Linus Torvalds was the original inspiration for the blanket clutching character in Charles M. Schultz's 'Peanuts' comic strip. The character of Lucy was based on Bill Gates.

An effective battery is made by using pineapple rings as the anode in a bath of washing up liquid as the cathode. A battery thus constructed of 1200 rings and eighteen gallons of washing up liquid will provide enough power to run three entire households for up to 36 hours. The use of high quality washing up liquid as opposed to cheap own brand will increase this by as many as three times. It's all to do with how long the bubbles last.

Gouging your own intestines out with a trowel will prevent the onset of mumps.

If you kill a 'Born again' Christian for awakening you too early on a Sunday morning, their corpses will burst into flames and rise phoenix like from their own ashes to become 'Born again again' Christians.

Not only do thirty per cent of Londoners believe that EastEnders is a fly-on-the-wall documentary series, but the same number believe that BBC News is a soap opera.

Anchovies can be dissolved in honey but not in a laboratory-made glucose syrup. This is how cheap fish flavoured toffees are made.

Dannii Minogue is Kylie's alter ego that has broken through from another universe.

The tales of Deputy Dawg and Mussky were based upon the real life antics at Paddington Green police station.

Angle grinders come in four types - acute, obtuse, right and reflex - depending on the type of work you need to do.

A scrotal abscess can be avoided by eating half your bodyweight in oranges daily.

Dodos were hunted to extinction not for their meat but because their stupid beaks offended the eyes of the travelling clergy.

'Cookies' stored on your computer by popular internet search engine Google have more chocolate chips than those stored by Yahoo.com.

96% of Americans are below average in every respect.

Camels refuse to accept the concept of an afterlife, believing that anything with sand, sun, two humps and the ability to produce spit that takes a week to wash out of hair must be in heaven already.

When Rolling Stones guitarist Keith Richards wants to relax he will only sit in a rocking chair.

Having a big nose is punishable by 40 lashes in Saudi Arabia as it is a sign of heresy.

Mobile phones transmit your exact position to Satan.

It is illegal to eat meat at designated 'meeting points' in British Museums and other tourist attractions.

The Flintstones were famously used to advertise Winston cigarettes in the 60s, and such clips can be found on the Internet. In the vaults, well hidden away, there are also test reels of adverts for the Flintstones advertising marijuana, as it was expected to be legalised in 1971. The advertising company thought the 'getting stoned/stone age' concept was an excellent advertising hook.

For the next series of the seemingly endless stream of reality TV shows, losers will face a firing squad - but 3 out of 5 times the squad will be firing blanks. In addition to the tears of disappointment from the unsuccessful participants, TV bosses hope to capture pant-wetting terror, screams for mercy and executions 40% of the time, for transmission as part of their tea-time televisual schedules.

Welsh Choral Singers can be easily identified by the tattoo of the logo of the band Blodwyn Pig, above the hairline at the nape of the neck.

Rowan Atkinson lives in fear of being left in the sun, lest he melt even more.

String theory has been abandoned by reputable physicists after its earliest proponents were found to be sponsored by the British String Manufacturer's Association.

All-girl rock band L7 were all leaders of G8 countries.

The best way to clear your sinuses is with a shotgun.

As of June 2006, all 'blind summits' which merit their own road sign will also have to have a guide dog permanently tied to the signpost.

It's a well-known fact that most 'Indian' meals served in British restaurants are nothing to do with real Indian cuisine. It's less well known that the allegedly Indian dish names translate as 'fuck off you ignorant bastards' in Urdu, Gujarati, Punjabi and indeed many of the less common languages from the Indian sub-continent.

Frequent and vigorous sex encourages hair growth in balding men.

Bleach is an effective douche. Parazone with its extra clingy tendencies works best of all.

The concept of the 'thousand yard stare' is based on a typographical error. It was originally a 'thousand yard snare' used by ambitious hunters who in keeping watch would have to oversee the five-eighths of a mile distance; hence the confusion. The stare referred to (the glassy eyed look into the distance) is rarely more than 150 feet.

Electricity can be stored in jars lined with kitchen foil. A 454g jar can store up to 700kW, enough to power a fridge-freezer for up to 15 days.

Hanging a baboon corpse from a light fitting in your bedroom will prevent the onset of ringworm.

You can get a grant from the Government if you stink of piss.

Right now there is a hit man within 800 yards of you prepared to 'permanently remove' someone on your behalf for a figure of no more than £1500. Guaranteed results within 7 days or your money back.

Freudian slips can be purchased in the underwear department of most branches of Marks and Spencer.

It can be mathematically proven that a stitch in time actually saves 9.3.

Microsoft's Terms & Conditions for every operating system since Windows Vista allows them access to your children for slavery purposes. These T&Cs are still better than those attached to any Apple products.

King Crimson was named after King Harold IV of Denmark, also known as Blushing Harold, noted for his stammer, tendency to sweat profusely, and general ill-ease around women.

It is recorded that for a sea battle against the Spanish on the first of April 1536, Henry VIII ordered his galleons to load up only rubber cannonballs 'to verily scare the shite from our enemies and have a good laugh at their expense.'

Just as technically a 'blue moon' is the second full moon in a calendar month, a 'black sabbath' is the thirteenth Sunday in any given calendar month.

Science has proven that a child's Christmas toy that costs less than a tenner will be played with and treasured forever, while those in excess of £100 will be discarded by Dec. 28th - although the box the toy came in will provide years of joy.

Bruce Forsyth moonlights from his golf-playing, playing card-swapping TV presenter persona as the death metal singer Mortiis.

According to a famous advert 'biting bubbles is better'. This is sadly not true as Bubbles is getting very fed up with the whole thing and has a nasty bite herself, to go with a wicked right hook.

Food items which rhyme also taste similar.

1960s push-button stereos had 'Volume Up' and 'Volume Down' buttons, marked 'Turn It Up Daddio' and 'Stop It Daddy, It Hurts' respectively.

The Battle of Bosworth Field, at which Richard III lost his crown to Henry Tudor (later Henry VII) kicked off because a 'mere knave' looked at Richard's mistress 'in a funny way'.

The original velocipede was a three foot long creature, similar to a centipede, but with a hundred little wheels instead of legs.

Popular 1980s computer game 'Chuckie Egg' was based on the life story of Karl Marx.

The phrase 'go to work on an egg' was originally coined by The Mork & Mindy Automobile Company.

The DNA of tofu is identical to the DNA of a Friesian cow - therefore it is meat.

Hit single 'Funky Town' by Lipps Inc. was written about Bolton, Lancashire.

White chocolate is made from melted down albino squirrels.

In the early 70s (before CDs were invented) experiments were carried out to determine the specifications for the best possible reproduction of sound from a vinyl record. Scientists deduced that the best reproduction came from a 12" record pressed on pure virgin vinyl specifically designed to play at 4000 rpm. The only downside was that the play duration was roughly eleven seconds and thus the medium was useless for anything but radio jingles. As a by-product, the 4000rpm jingle for Radio Norfolk when played at 33rpm through an underwater speaker system was apparently a clarion call to whales to beach themselves and die in an act of senseless nobility; hence the rash of such occurrences in 1975.

Bill Ward has been voted 'Funniest Member of Black Sabbath Ever' thanks to a joke he told in 1975 about fish. Ronnie James Dio was voted 'Most Ridiculous', beating Bev Bevan by a single vote.

Impressionist artists of the late 19th century did their best works while drunk.

Word games are for nerds.

Charles Dickens wrote his first novel 'The Pickwick Papers' on a series of gin bottle labels, stored on a clothes line, attached by clothes pegs. The first three chapters were written in his own blood and the rest would have been had he not developed septicaemia from the bloodletting and had a quill donated by a kindly cotton mill owner while he was recovering. There is a missing chapter that should slot between chapters 3 and 4, entitled 'Delusions, delirium and soiling the bed in fevered fear'.

Hungarians are three times more gullible than other Europeans.

In its 2005 TV schedules, Channel 5 announced several ground-breaking new programmes, including 'When Pastry Chefs Go Bad', 'Britain's Greatest Asbestos Removal Accidents' and '100 Things You Never Knew About Boils'. Every single one was cancelled before transmission.

The policeman on duty outside 10 Downing Street is armed with a crossbow.

As silicone hardens it increases in density. By 2012, Jordan's breasts were each expected to weigh as much as a walrus and to require transport in slings supported by wheeled frames but she had them swapped out for helium.

The most popular pub name in England is 'The Perforated Fridge'. No-one knows why.

The most comprehensive Swiss Army Knife ever released (in 1983) contained 381 devices, including CB antenna, dog polisher and Polaroid camera. It was twenty-one inches long and weighed twenty six pounds, and only three were ever sold, two of those to Jonathan King.

Robbie Williams was born in the future.

Most great works of fiction start out as factual reference books, but this aspect of the book is generally abandoned when the author realises the depth of research required.

Not only did Herbie Flowers write the song 'Granddad' - he also scripted the children's TV series of the same name.

It is forbidden to transport English 'Real Ales' to countries in the Middle East as they contain technology which could be used as weaponry.

Polio tastes faintly of mint.

In the wild, bottlenose dolphins are really miserable. They only acquire their smiley faces and happy demeanours when captured and brought to live in big swimming pools at SeaWorld-type entertainment complexes.

The chief flavouring ingredient in a Mars Bar is hedgehog vomit.

Eamonn Holmes wears a fat suit to appear on TV; in reality he weighs just six and a half stones. Lorraine Kelly on the other hand dresses in a compression chamber to force her twenty-six stones into her size 14 dresses under pressures of up to 300psi.

Windows 2003 Server had the codename 'SkyNet' when it was being created. It was expected to take over the world and unleash a horde of killer droids in 2010 but Microsoft issued a patch fix to deal with it.

If you're ever short of Tippex, Artex makes a fine substitute, and will never be noticed.

Jabba the Hutt was born in Newport, South Wales.

Jonathan King was released early from prison in order to make room in the nonce wing for Michael Jackson. Alas for the foresight of the governor of that establishment.

The Christian religious service 'vespers' is so named because the priesthood are all required to arrive on Italian motor scooters, as our Lord did in at the Garden of Gethsemane.

Scientists have developed a very rare blue goldfish to make the head-flushed-down-toilet schoolboy prank more viable.

'Where do they make balloons?' is a question asked in song by popular group 'They Might Be Giants'. If they'd only asked one of the members of less popular group 'The Balloon Farm', they'd have found out, as party balloons are indeed grown on giant farms in the outback of Australia.

A garden shed is both tax-deductible and will provide 100% protection from meteor strikes.

The first cats were originally sold as merchandising on the back of the runaway success of Tom and Jerry cartoons.

Tony Blair changed his surname by deed poll in 1978. He was originally called Tony Ubermensch.

Guitar teachers with a recording history only ever teach the tracks they played on.

84% of all magazines available today are utterly spurious. Hence 84% of 'media people' would better serve humankind by either going on the dole or committing suicide.

The moon is a hundred miles away from Earth.

Popular seventies family car the Austin Allegro was made by gently squashing a Bentley Corniche in a scrapyard crusher, then hammering out most of the dents.

Renee Zellweger is hollow and is getting thinner as she slowly deflates.

Members of the House of Lords are honour-bound to deliver a pepperoni and anchovy pizza to your door if you ring them up and ask for one. This is why most of them keep their telephone numbers ex-directory.

Tesco supermarkets recently experimented with the sale of 'Bedfordshire' cheese, until it was pointed out that they had been duped by an unscrupulous farmer, and the 'cheese' was in fact horse manure.

Feeding surplus Viagra tablets to your dog will give it the uncanny ability to speak Welsh and juggle cabbages for at least fifteen minutes.

Nokia mobile telephones have since 2004 been able to contact aliens from the planet Neptune. The option can be found just after 'Fire gamma ray death beam' in the menu.

In 1995 an illegal artificial insemination clinic near Coventry was closed down after dissatisfied clients claimed to police that their eggs had not only been mixed up with those of other couples, but that the clinic had used wallpaper paste to fertilise them.

Flags were banned from the 'Guantanamo Bay Detention Centre' illegal prisoner of war ritualised abuse camp and unlawful Geneva Convention violation shithole, to stop 'prisoners' communicating with anyone by semaphore. They managed it anyway with their trouser legs.

Hamsters live longer if you power them with Ni-Cad batteries.

Tower blocks are haunted by the dead who live in the foundations.

Authority and perversity correlate. There's a good chance your boss does it with animals.

The next big thing in alternative music will be Straight Emo, a hybrid of straight edge and emocore, in which songs about lost girlfriends are played until the audience is in tears, but the audience will then beat itself up for being weak and dependent upon another.

The last Labour Government briefly considered a plan to rename the counties of England as '1', '2', '3', '4' etc. as it seemed more logical. Leicestershire was pencilled in as number 14.

Second rate actor Mr T, controversial rapper Ice-T and ex-Radio 1 DJ DLT are brothers.

Most people are aware that the last King of Albania was called Zog, but very few know that the last-but-one was called Goosegrease.

Computers work by tri-cubic induction. No-one in the world knows how tri-cubic induction works.

Lief Ericcson was born in a tree.

DJ and singer duo 'Chaka Demus and Pliers' were originally called 'Chaka Demus and Woodrasp'.

The most often attempted style of self-harm by teenagers is biting their own elbows.

Old ladies who are both rich and vain can grow Pomeranians out of their armpits.

Janet Jackson was a manifestation of her brother's transvestite tendencies.

The 14th Earl of Sandwich invented the pork pie.

The Muppets were animated by putting very small antelopes into furry suits.

Mucus is a sedative; this is why the sharpest thinkers are often dry-mouthed.

God died in 1973 in Kentucky USA after being beaten up by some farm hands for 'wearing a long white dress'. The four farm hands were fined $25 each and lightly chastised for 'killing a hippy', deemed to be a crime of the same magnitude as a speeding ticket at the time.

'Grandma We Love You' by The St. Winifred's School Choir if played at half speed in reverse is an exhortation to the Dark Lord to rise up and kill the weak and frail.

Television DIY 'experts' frequently recommend the use of breeze blocks if you're ever short of glass for a window pane.

Methylated Spirit and off brand cola is available as a pre-mixed drink (or 'alcopop') in higher class drinking establishments in South East London.

Cocaine can be easily refined from ordinary household bleach.

Publishing sensation 'Mein Kampf' was written by Mister Ed, the talking horse. Mister Ed was later prosecuted for inciting racial hatred but escaped the electric chair on a technicality.

In 2003 Sunderland achieved a suicide rate of 1023 people per thousand; a statistical anomaly that came about by people moving to the city and not even making the whole year before ending it all in misery and desperation.

Michael Douglas is operated by wires and pulleys which are controlled by Catherine Zeta Jones' brain patterns via a piece of electronic equipment loosely based on a Texas Instruments calculator.

Israeli prime ministers are chosen specifically to present a challenge to BBC newsreaders.

Vulcanised rubber is made by baking cheese in a medium oven (gas mark 4).

Sticking toast to walls with peanut butter will help you pass exams in accountancy, law and French Literature, but not geography.

At least half of all craft fairs in the UK now accept stalls selling Kraftwerk t-shirts and CDs.

It is entirely possible to build viable wings for humans from Post-It notes.

Marbles was originally played with dog eggs, as was conkers.

The favoured weapon of the Thuggee, the silent assassins of fourteenth century India, was the Sten gun.

Cruelty to animals is the national sport of Denmark.

Smoking dried badger will give you scrapie.

Repeatedly phoning directory enquiries will get you a telegram from the Queen.

King Alfred may have burnt the cakes but simultaneously invented the barbecue, a name derived from the Norse 'burbekue' meaning 'charred to a crisp'.

There are only three different species of fish. All the others are done with mirrors.

Nu-metal halfwits Slipknot are all named after characters in children's TV series, 'Willo the Wisp'.

Leslie Ash's lips were, at their peak, pumped up to more than 80psi. Lynne Perrie's were at a record breaking 110psi for three minutes before they exploded in a shower of hot silicone and lard.

Copper wire is made by stretching policemen out really, really thinly.

The black and white striped kit associated with Newcastle United FC was originally used because all the team members were fond of mint humbugs.

Just as IBM started out making typewriters, Sun Microsystems started out making electric wheelchairs.

Petrol can be diluted with malt vinegar in a ratio of up to one part petrol to three of vinegar. Diesel can only be diluted with sunflower oil, and then only up to 1:1 ratio. Both are inherently environmentally friendly.

Edward Woodward lives in fear of vowels being outlawed.

The EU Supreme Court has decreed that the crime of 'fraud' should be renamed 'creative accounting' so as not to offend the criminal or as they should now be known, 'victim'.

Self-denial is a form of nagging when practised by wives.

The earliest action photographs were of projectiles hitting tea sets; hence the phrase 'mug shot'. When the Police Council met in 1927 to name the photographs taken of suspected criminals, the considered it to be a better name than the other alternative, 'cum shot', a variant on 'crim shot'.

Eating bread crusts does not give you curly hair. It actually gives you curly legs.

New England doesn't exist anywhere but on the National Geographic channel. It was created to cheer people up and make them hope they might not live out their days in Orpington.

Kabbalah texts only allow seven 'accepted holy' varieties of penguin. The rest are thus deemed to be Creations of Satan, and these include Adelie and Little Blue, primarily because they're not as aesthetically pleasing as Emperor or Rockhopper.

Crack cocaine is a cheap and effective substitute for chillies.

Canine teeth are so called because they're implanted by surgeons into new-borns, the teeth coming from recently deceased dogs.

The concept of the brass band was invented by the Spanish Inquisition as a method of extracting confessions from heretics.

Bavarian laws state that a beer glass should not be less than two pints but a coffee cup may not contain more than three sips.

Damian Hirst's next project is to preserve half of Tracey Emin in formaldehyde.

The average household fridge contains enough freon to power York for a month, if used in a freon - plutonium converter and atomic pile. Modern fridges contain a small atomic pile to fully utilise this freon, which is why they don't have a plug.

Model and cocaine fiend Kate Moss is made of driftwood and twigs.

The first muffins were tuna flavoured, despite having no fish derived ingredients.

Arnold Schwarzenegger's muscles are produced by a 'Pink Panther' style inflatable suit.

The original lyrics to Underworld's 'Born Slippy' anthem (as used in the film 'Trainspotting') were 'Courage Directors, Marston's Pedigree, Timothy Taylor Landlord, Theakston Old Peculiar', but they couldn't get it to scan.

The amount of nine carat gold worn outside the clothing by an individual is inversely proportionate to their IQ. Gold bought at Elizabeth Dukes at Argos gets double points.

An ancient by-law in Chester requires the dropper of chewing gum to be 'smote with mighty thunderbolts'.

'A Heated Debate' is a popular brand of bed warmer in Japan.

All past winners of TV quiz show 'Going for Gold' have been professional drummers.

There is a diner just outside Des Moines, Iowa, staffed by James Dean, Marilyn Monroe, Elvis Presley and Jim Morrison. Most recent addition is Johnny Cash, but because he's the new boy he'll be mopping floors until another rock or silver screen legend allegedly dies.

King Canute, properly spelt Cnut, was a typographical error. His real name was David Johannsen, and through reincarnation he became the singer with the New York Dolls.

There is only one station on the London Underground that has a name that contains all the consonants. It's Highbury and Islington.

BONJOUR,
MOTHERF*CKERS

Fear of badgers is fast becoming a Europe-wide epidemic.

It's known that sweet corn passes through the bowel undigested. What's less well known is that as it passes through the digestive tract it actively sucks all happiness from the host, leaving a sad, hollowed shell of a man, his life destroyed by the apathy and self-loathing only sweet corn ingestion can imbue.

The website 'snopes.com' which debunks popular urban myths found on the internet is actually run as a joint venture by the CIA, the Bavarian Illuminati, the Freemasons and the British Royal

Family in order to stop people finding out what really goes on in the world.

Mark Twain's quote that 'Golf is a good walk spoiled' was originally 'Golf - why? Bastard squirrels' and was first said in the Clubhouse of the Knotty Pines Golf Course after a game in which the local wildlife stole his ball.

In some parts of the U.S. it is illegal to call a spade a spade.

'Hell hath no fury like a woman scorned' the popular phrase tells us. In fact Hell has had no fury at all since it ran out in 2003, having deposited all fury upon the face of the planet, principally in the Mid-West where it had the effect of infuriating right wing Christians into condemning everything without exception as 'unholy' or 'un-American', including churches, the Bible and Jimmy Swaggart.

Muffin the Mule, Andy Pandy, and Lady Rosemary from The Herbs were cold war spies for the Soviets. They fled London with Burgess and MacLean, taking documents proving their ownership of their respective hit television shows with them. The shows are never repeated, as to do so would channel funds into the Russian Communist Party.

Ulan Bator, the capital of Mongolia, was named after the local name for their most prevalent sexually transmitted disease in the region, syphilis.

It is theoretically impossible for fish to swim.

'Green' aerosols have been invented but they are powered by horse flatulence and the side effects of such a propulsion system are not regarded as positives.

'Hai Karate' was named after the cry of the drunken fighter outside a thousand pubs across the land trying to scare his opponent into backing down. The reality of course is that the cry of 'hai! karate!' means 'I haven't the first clue but maybe you'll be fooled.' A kicking generally ensues.

White mice conduct electricity better than copper does.

Ballet dancers are better than ninjas at conkers.

Woolwich Arsenal was originally a storage house for body parts required for colon transplant surgery.

Playing computer games will make you radioactive enough to cook a chicken merely by standing next to it.

In the nativity play at Nazareth C of E Infants, Jesus played 'Third Botulism Carrier'.

Delia Smith's recipe for bacon sandwiches contains no bacon whatsoever.

Fritz Lang's masterpiece of 1927, 'Metropolis', was actually filmed in 1861, 21 years before the Parisian Etienne Jules Marey invented the cine camera. Lang kept it on the shelf for so long because he couldn't explain why he had a time machine that HG Wells had lost in 1899, shortly after finishing his book of the same name.

The mawkishness of British newspapers is proportional to the distance from London of an accident, divided by the number of British victims. Foreign victims score no points.

Among the non-existent objects believed in by Austrian philosopher Alexius Minong were the three headed wildebeest, the hemispherical golf ball, the eight dimensional hamster cage and the Zippo Combined Cigarette Lighter / Trouser Press.

William Hedley's Puffing Billy, the famous locomotive engine, was originally going to be named the Steaming Pantload.

A recent nine-page article in New Scientist magazine has revealed that while Einstein was setting out to disprove quantum theory he accidentally proved that eight was less than three. This research has been covered up for years.

An old wives' cure for haemorrhoids is to take a piece of cheese, rub it on the afflicted area, and then serve it in a sandwich to a disliked aunt.

Bat spit is ounce-for-ounce more valuable than cocaine because of its restorative qualities - a pound of bat spit can reverse aging by thirty years.

Black computer pixels are made from octopus ink.

Pouring boiling lead into your ears is a safe and inexpensive method of ear wax removal.

Filling your kettle with gravel will make your cups of tea taste of honey.

Store loyalty cards are a form of indoctrination into the dark arts.

While many people are aware that the saxophone was invented by a Belgian, Adolph Sax, fewer people know that many other musical instruments were invented by Belgians. Examples include Herman Vibro, Geoffrey Trom, Werner von Flugel and Willi Bagpi, inventor of the bagpipes.

Office water coolers are mind control devices in disguise. The water within is laced with highly addictive drugs to entice you back for more mind control.

Due to an injunction taken out in 1977 Jimmy Savile was not permitted within 30 yards of Kenny Everett's grave for fear he would have danced on it.

John the Baptist was actually a Methodist.

The Morris Minor car was originally intended to be driven underground as it would dissolve in direct sunlight.

The US Senate is wholly owned by McDonalds.

Estonia's nuclear deterrent is computer controlled by a Commodore 64.

In certain parts of the Midlands it is traditional to disembowel a dead badger with a spade upon the event of one's birthday.

Kraft Foods, manufacturers of Cheez Whiz, also trialled the less well known foods 'Tomato Dope', 'Lentil Smack' and 'Banana Gak'.

The New Musical Express, popularly known as the NME, started life as the Northamptonshire Mutton Eater, a small focus magazine containing nothing but sheep meat recipes and stories of muttoncentric dinner parties.

Kurt Cobain's 'suicide' was actually a failed attempt to take extreme trepanning to the next level.

It is illegal for any children's video cassette or DVD to have a running time of more than 62 minutes, regardless of the capacity of the medium.

The Milky Bar Kid was lactose intolerant.

German cheese makers are required to sit yearly exams on specialist subjects of their choice at the German equivalent of A level (minimum), as long as they're in no way relevant to cheese. The German government is keenly aware that their cheese is seen as being stupid next to the French and wants to improve their image. 82% of applicants fail the Cheese Common Entrance examinations.

The 1904 Olympics featured 'Being cruel to animals' as a demonstration sport.

Schadenfreude is German for 'shit friend'.

Fresh dog intestines make the most effective temporary replacement fan belt should yours snap. This effect also works in reverse. Should your dog's small intestine snap it can be replaced with a fan belt, available at any branch if Halfords.

In 1987 Marvel Comics released a short lived series of comic books based around the adventures of a masked superhero called The Hillman Avenger.

The Queen may not vote due to an outstanding county court judgement against her.

Birmingham was built as a prison for criminals whose crime didn't warrant transportation to Australia.

Popular American stadium rock act Cheap Trick is so named because they only charge ten dollars and 15 cents (plus beers) to perform.

None of the members of Talk Talk could speak.

People over six feet tall can reach out and touch the moon if they stand on tiptoes.

The Mamas And The Papas started life as an indie-punk grunge band in the same vein as Husker Du, fifteen years ahead of their time. They went under the moniker Scrotal Abscess and released one 7" single 'Death In The Flowers' b/w 'Ultra Psychotic Drug Machine' on the Barking Starfish label of San Francisco. The volte face happened when they swapped amphetamines for acid.

The highest score possible with three darts on a standard dartboard is actually two hundred and seventeen.

Balti dishes in Indian restaurants are traditionally cooked in one of those Second World War German helmets that had ear flaps.

Girls who wear braces on their teeth find magnets attractive.

Scientists still cannot explain the fleeting popularity of Tiffany in the mid-80s.

Enid Blyton had a series of pornographic novels lined up for submission to her publisher when she died, all involving her earlier creations the Famous Five, Secret Seven and Five Find-Outers (and Dog). Every one included bestiality, necrophilia and coprophilia but very little 'straight' sex.

Robert Kilroy-Silk eats eight pounds of raw carrots a day to maintain his bizarre complexion.

The first mobile telephones were actually food mixers with added loudspeakers. Calls could only be made by shouting into the blender attachment.

Robert Mugabe, the insane ultra-fascist political leader of Zimbabwe, rates his top three historical figures as Stalin, Mengele, and the taller of the Chuckle Brothers.

Dead pets can have their hearts restarted by a car battery charger that is set for 'fast charge' from the mains if the positive crocodile clip is attached around the neck of the deceased creature and the negative to the tail.

In Alabama a tortoise is required to get planning permission every spring ahead of enlarging its shell.

Three of The Nolan Sisters were men.

Jeremy Clarkson was born Judith Chalmers. He sometimes still moonlights as his previous persona (pre-op) but isn't very convincing. The name change meant he could keep all the monogrammed hankies, dressing gowns etc.

Popular 1960s group leader Dave Clark couldn't count. This is proven by the fact that there were forty-three members of the Dave Clark 5, all of whom played the French horn.

Having a technical book on your bookshelf is exactly the same as being an expert on the subject.

Korean is Chinese when you're drunk.

Early dictionaries had words listed in a totally arbitrary order. It was only at the start of the 20th century that words began to be placed in alphabetical order.

It a contractual obligation of all one hit wonders from 1978 to 1996 that they will, post-fame, spend at least three years working in a DIY warehouse type of retail outlet. The rule was rescinded in 1996 when Simon Cowell thought of Pop Idol, and replaced 'DIY retail outlet' with 'plebeian clothing retailer'.

Despite being published monthly the last time anyone bought a copy of 'Fretwork Monthly - The Woodworking Jamboree' was in September 1987. The purchaser was a bored guitarist who failed to read the strap line.

Margaret Thatcher had a tattoo of Stalin on her left buttock.

In the first draft of the Bible the number of the beast was fourteen.

There are thousands of novels written by rabbits which are better than Joseph Heller's 'Catch 22', but they will never be seen on the shelves of your local branch of Waterstones due to an anti-lapine conspiracy among Zionist book publishers.

The TV series 'Quantum Leap' was inspired by the 70s children's' show 'Mr Benn'.

At birth, penguins can fly. Vets have to clip their wings to make them lose this ability.

Ozzy Osbourne was stalking the Earth as the rotting undead until his quad bike accident in which he spontaneously came back to life.

Jeffrey Barnard is recorded in the Guinness Book of World Records as being the healthiest human being ever.

The Queen is her own twin sister. That's why she has two birthdays.

Damon Hill votes Jesuit.

The showroom dummies in popular clothing store Marks and Spencer are exact replicas of Jonathan Ross (male) and Hermann Goering (female).

Many childhood tantrums are caused by fundamental disagreements with religious doctrine and an expression thereof. Children usually grow out of them by the age of three, learning to accept other faiths.

The golf clubs known as 'drivers' are so called because they all have second jobs working for a minicab firm in Plaistow, East London.

Levitating goats became extinct in the nineteenth century when they got so good at it they levitated out of the atmosphere and suffocated.

The advent of the 'flat' plasma screen television has forced TV companies to develop flat actors to fit inside. Old 'deep cased' TVs contained sufficient space to lodge 300 popular four inch high actors. They get out of the back at night for a walk around the lounge - this is why a TV in the bedroom is a creepy, eerie thing.

It is physically impossible for a chicken to tango; their legs aren't bendy enough.

The largest muscle in the human body is the arse-shouting cord.

27% of global warming is caused by excess electricity use at Christmas in pursuit of the 'Gaudiest And Most Tasteless House Lighting Display In The Western World' award.

Odd-numbered holes on golf courses are home to little pixies, who constantly complain about the fact that they can't get planning permission for a new roof as 'it's against club rules'.

The Crimean War was invented by Florence Nightingale as a promotional campaign for Smith & Wesson.

Before toasters were invented the only way to cook bread was to pop it in the microwave.

Surbiton is fictional, created by Dante as his sixth level of Hell. The seventh is Chorleywood.

A cup of sweet tea (300ml, 2 sugars) is sufficient to sustain an earwig for eight years.

Certain parts of the UK, specifically in remoter parts of Derbyshire and around the Wash, are still in black and white.

Hans Blix invented several types of stickers used in offices.

God maintains a daily 'blog, where he pontificates about Linux, Web 2.0, why he can't get a girlfriend, and the deeper meaning of Star Wars movies.

Bleach is an excellent substitute for lemon squash. The bleach must obviously be unflavoured.

A picture paints exactly 834 words, contrary to the well-known phrase. Dyslexia suffers get a free 20% bonus.

VoIP phones send your voice into the sixth dimension for transmission. They can be rendered ineffectual by wrapping in tin foil smeared with marmalade.

John Merrick (aka: The Elephant Man) did not kill himself as portrayed in the film - rather, he joined BBC local radio as a newsreader.

Mobile phone battery life can be extended by up to three weeks by plugging the phone directly into the mains rather than going through the wussy converter. If your phone's man enough it'll cope.

A diet of bananas and eggs is healthier than a diet of prunes, figs and malt cake.

The term 'constipated' has been deemed un-PC by Lambeth Borough Council. The approved term is to be 'excrementally challenged'.

The world's finest cheese is made from the sweat from a baboon's arse.

Brussels sprouts served al dente are hazardous to health since when not cooked right through '60s style there is a risk that an unfortunate diner may bite on a bullet secreted in the green death vegetable.

Under the 1992 Disabilities Act every office is forced to have one employee who is unaware of their devastating body odour problem. In some cases companies can actually get grants to maintain persons who reek of onions regardless of their actual productivity.

Garnier's 'Paris laboratory' is a bedsit occupied by one of their junior technicians near to the Champs Elysees. It's equipped with a 'Young Scientist' chemistry set, a single gas hob to act as a Bunsen burner and 800 empty Pot Noodle containers.

The energy expended in digesting fresh semen exceeds the calorific value of the fluid. The natural conclusion is that women on diets - or even those looking to maintain a trim figure - should seek to ingest as much fresh semen as possible.

If stored with one end in water, cotton wool buds eventually burst into cotton wool flowers.

Fuzzy logic is an expansion kit for Fuzzy Felt, marketed to child prodigies.

Jesus actually said 'Numismatists will inherit the earth'. He couldn't stand the meek and thought they were whining victim syndromic bastards.

David Beckham and Victoria 'Posh Spice' Adams met at the University Challenge semi-finals 1994. Both were working as stagehands, shifting scenery.

Doors were only invented as a by-product of the hinge industry.

Bone china can only be effectively cleaned by shot-blasting it.

Wee Jimmy Krankie was born a boy but lost his genitalia in a bizarre gardening accident aged 7, hence the distressing transvestite/paedophile stage 'act'.

Cheese is milk, frozen in time.

Former United States President George 'Dubya' Bush can see into the future in eight different alternate universes. Unfortunately none of them are this one.

'O' and 'A' level exams were named after popular prostitute services.

Cigarettes are nicknamed 'snouts' because they were originally glued closed with pig mucus.

Ron Jeremy as a schoolboy wanted to be a Master Baker but his careers master was alas slightly hard of hearing and got him on a somewhat different work experience week. He never looked back.

A rift in the space-time continuum once gave a Countdown contestant a 13 letter word, 'fundamentally', despite there only being nine characters on the board.

It is not true that Henry VIII had six wives. This misconception is due to a misprint in a contemporary church document. In fact, King Hal was half-cat, and had six lives.

Winnits, or 'arse sultanas' are actually piles (or 'bum grapes') that have been left out in the sun.

Football manager and pundit Terry Venables is based on an amalgam of three characters in EastEnders.

Data mining used to be a manual task carried out by men with code chisels and fact barrows several hundred metres beneath the Earth's surface. The stat donkeys used to pull the data wagons frequently didn't see daylight for several years at a time, bathed instead in the light of a million LEDs on a thousand UNIX servers.

Children can win a Victoria Cross by default if they can run across the M4 six times in thirty seconds in daylight.

European Law decrees that all ear trumpets must be tuned to concert 'A'.

The collective noun for lies is a 'spunk'.

Books burn better on bonfires in Birmingham.

Stones with holes in them float in water.

The reading of tabloid newspapers has directly contributed to the average IQ of a mob falling to 63, down from 71 in 1985.

Dame Judi Dench was born Harold Faltermeyer and composed 'Axel F' for Beverley Hills Cop before an experiment involving a sex change and a time machine.

Rod Hull was actually an ingenious hand puppet, operated by a big blue bird.

Geri Halliwell and Victoria Beckham are both early adopters of the Inverse Publicity Value Concept in which those persons who achieve the most publicity have the least talent and/or personability. Geri's talents for example appear to be having breasts, wearing clothes two sizes too small, and grinning like an escaped psychotic bunny boiler consumed by greed which, while all repulsive, garner her hundreds of column inches in the tabloid press yearly. Victoria's skills are sulking, being ridiculously thin and proving that people with IQs of less than 2 can exist outside of an iron lung. Again, the presence of Victoria on the sleeve of a weekly trash magazine has increased sales by up to 50,000 copies, despite her having no redeeming qualities of any kind. The IPVC has been promoted by such TV shows as Big Brother, Pop Idol and The X Factor and is fully accepted by that part of the population that holds soap operas as aspirational and fanciful.

Popular entertainer and renowned homosexual Elton John has a dairy farm in his navel.

Status Quo's early album 'Dog of Two Head' was named after a genetic experiment carried out by Francis Rossi while still at school.

The first pornographic magazine was published 45 minutes after the invention of the camera, but it took another 47 years before the introduction of the Readers' Wives pages, when cameras became more commonplace.

The laws of physics state that a Belgian man in his pyjamas on the surface of the planet cannot exceed 58 mph (93 km/h), and nor can any item to which he is attached. This is why so many overnight trains in Europe run late, but the daytime trains are seemingly not affected.

Morris dancing only became popular in the 1960s, after the decline in popularity of Bentley promenading and Alvis traipsing.

Leo Sayer is a reincarnation of Leonardo da Vinci.

Tennis was originally devised as a method of trench warfare, further development of which gave rise to the mortar.

In the vast majority of cases the damage wreaked by a bullet entering the body is an allergic reaction to the alloy from which the shell is made. The bullet itself would be travelling sufficiently fast as to pass through the body without disturbing any of the atoms. On TV they use bullets made from stainless steel to which no-one has an allergic reaction which explains why no-one ever 'got shot' on the A Team.

The best business decisions are those made on the grounds of who gives out the best freebies.

Modern cameras contain a device to force a person's eyes half closed before the shutter operates.

'Da Doo Ron Ron', a hit single for the Crystals was written about football manager Ron Atkinson's speech impediment.

Having a mobile phone that can record audio, play MP3s and movies, take high resolution photos, surf the Net, play games, make video calls and remote control your TV proves you're King Dork Of The Dorkonauts. Oh, that's everyone then. Shows how things have progressed since *that* was first written eh? ☺

Elaine Page was born as Bernard Bresslaw.

Jackson Pollock did it for a laugh. He was taking the piss. All his mates knew, but a bottle of scotch apiece at Christmas kept them schtum.

Cisco (the IT comms giant) was founded by the members of the '70s band Ottowan. Their first hit was to have been called C.I.S.C.O but someone at the record company inadvertently 'corrected' the title.

White chocolate Kit-Kats contain mouse semen.

Cheese is a state of mind as opposed to a dairy product.

People with ginger hair live longer if they're immersed in boiling tar once a week.

Iceland was once a Scottish island but was towed away in 1963 to fill up a blank bit of ocean. The Isle of Man is due for relocation to the outer edge of the Bay of Biscay in 2019 when local property prices will rocket.

The Isle of Wight is a giant pile of fossilized dinosaur droppings, probably from a Stegosaurus.

The turtle dove is so named due to its constant need to defecate.

China is attached to the rest of Asia by three and a half million mooring ropes. They are renewed on an 18 month rolling cycle.

'Drinking and Shouting' was an Olympic event in 2012 in East London. It's the local #1 sport.

Canaletto's extraordinarily detailed paintings of Venetian street scenes were originally all published in one book entitled 'Where's Luigi?'

Electricity is delivered by the movement of electrons. Those electrons reaching your light bulb now have taken on average 46 days to get there from the power station, at an average of 300 metres per hour down 33kW lines and only 28cm per hour in your house's wiring circuits. This is why it's dangerous to touch live electric wires; they're full of electrons! When new (empty) wires are plugged in, it takes up to three hours for the wires to become fully charged, though the initial trickle is often enough to power your appliances.

David Blunkett's dog was made from Lego, and was guided by radio control waves emanating from Gordon Brown's false leg.

Alien spaceships seen over the Nevada desert are huge extra-terrestrial off-world gambling dens, crammed wall to wall with strange fruit machines and Human Invaders video games.

Cuckoo clocks are built by hordes of very small demons in the third level of Hades. The 'Cuck-coo' noise is actually a rallying call for all black magicians within earshot.

Gravel tastes better after marinating in a seaweed broth.

BECAUSE NORMAL SPIDERS WEREN'T SCARY ENOUGH.

Spiders did not always spin webs. In fact, up until around ten thousand years ago they used to catch prey by chasing it down and hitting it with very small spiked clubs. However they then got the idea of spinning webs from mice. Interestingly, mice appear to have evolved further and there is no longer any species of mouse that spin webs; they have invented very small assault rifles with which they hunt for food. Those little crunchy bits you sometimes find in your loaf of bread? Mouse bullets.

The Old English letter þ (pronounced 'th' and called 'thorn') was abandoned in the eighteenth century when it was realised that the semaphore signal for it was physically impossible.

Most chutneys were outlawed by Oliver Cromwell, which is why rabbit, beaver and fenugreek chutneys are not more prevalent today.

Men's brains typically fill up by the age of 32, women's at 37. This is because men memorise more useless trivia.

Computers generate random numbers for computer games and other applications by ringing Jeffrey Archer and asking him in which year he was born.

Charles Dickens' monthly pamphlet releases of his books chapter by chapter, far from being highly collectable were the Viz or Auto Trader of their day and were frequently kept in the lavatory or used to line budgie cages.

'Kangaroo' is the Aboriginal Australian word for 'Bob Beaman? Ha ha ha!'

Abandoned coal mines will ooze curds from the rock face if kept moist.

You can make a really tasty soup using prosthetic limbs as the primary ingredient.

Emigrating cures cataracts.

The domain name 'michaeljacksonisakiddyfiddler.com' and all variations of it (.co.uk, .net etc.) were owned by Jackson himself, in order to make a fortune selling merchandise should he ever be convicted.

Boils are a message from God urging you to commit murder.

Sausage rolls were invented before either sausages, or sausage meat.

Geinerwetramminer is a cheese from Bavaria made of wheat and oysters.

Bluetooth headsets turn your teeth green.

The original line-up of Motörhead was: Carol Vorderman (bass and vocals), Bruce Forsythe (drums) and Pope John Paul I (guitar). Lemmy was just a roadie.

Counting sheep at night will not only help you get to sleep but will also enter you for all Reader's Digest prize draws from now until Doomsday.

Thirty minutes' viewing of Star Trek (any variant) will reduce the sperm count of the average male by 76%. 100% depletion occurs at fifty-seven minutes.

The highest fee ever paid to a tribute band for a single performance is £322,000, paid by Camden Council to have their 2003 Christmas party guests entertained by 'The Counterfeit Exploited'.

Shoes were invented by Queen Victoria in 1896. Prior to this invaluable invention British people could only keep their feet dry in winter by sporting a pair of galoshes.

During times of famine many cream cakes are filled with snow as a cheap cream substitute.

Most IT Directors think IT stands for Interspatial Transmission and believe their job involves watching lots of Star Trek.

Botulism was originally a diet aid until 1964 when it was superseded by Slimfast. Negative publicity from the Slimfast advert people has given botulism its bad name today.

Children's glue is made from the dead pets of the very same children; a cruel trick of fate.

The sky is held aloft by swarms of starlings with clouds tied to their feet, working in shifts.

Coca-Cola contains embalming fluid.

Cats urinate around your house to repel evil spirits.

In one year the average human will shed enough skin cells to replace three square yards of flesh. Scientists are working on gathering these cells, and growing them for skin grafts and the like. They envisage being able to buy skin on a 50 metre roll, about a foot wide and like Sellotape, only with less tendency to stick to itself.

Wayne Rooney has undergone several dozen hours plastic surgery to achieve his Shrek-like appearance. Prior to going under the knife he closely resembled Cary Grant.

Smoking four cigarettes simultaneously and constantly for a full 24 hours will result in an automatic qualification for a Victoria Cross, a new clean driving license and a hereditary title with a seat in the House of Lords.

Just as the University of Huddersfield was upgraded from being mere Huddersfield Polytechnic, Cambridge University was until 1963 Cambridge C of E Infants School.

Manna, referred to in Biblical writings as spiritual nourishment of divine origin, was made up of sherbet lemons and Asda own brand crisps.

CDs were originally manufactured as cheap weapons for ninja. Their data storage properties were discovered completely by accident.

Opposable thumbs were originally treated with suspicion.

Until 1974 The Isle of Man was propelled by a 400hp Perkins diesel engine, taking tourists on extended touring holidays around the Irish Sea. When it broke down the anchor was dropped and it has remained moored in position ever since.

The Observers Book of Birds was written and illustrated in its entirety by Edward Lear.

Monty Python was a 19th century ornithologist, but is only acknowledged by the comedy troupe of the same name in their 'Albatross' sketch.

Popular children's film 'Mary Poppins' is based on the life and times of Jackie Kennedy. Walt Disney personally OK'd the removal of all references to Greek shipping magnates from the script, and added the umbrella powered flying scenes after a long session in the pub.

Elbows were an optional extra on babies until 1943.

Choosing to study Chemistry at university is a social faux-pas on a par with the public admission of paedophilia.

MSN Messenger is actually just a rebranded Pony Express.

'Sarcasm is the lowest form of wit' is a popular phrase but it is alas inaccurate. The lowest form of wit is Jim Davidson.

Mulberries are cranberries grown on the Isle of Mull.

Jesuit priests were often mistaken for trees until they changed their uniforms from a bark/leaves ensemble to something warmer and drier.

The Church of England was invented by Henry VIII to win a bet with the Pope.

Helmut Kohl, the 32nd Chancellor of Germany (6th of the Federal Republic), was born Helmut von Klinkerhoffen but changed his name by deed poll when the TV series 'Allo Allo' because popular. He named himself after an item in his wife's makeup bag. Similarly, Gerhard Schroeder's original surname was Fallenmaddonich, (as in '...with the big boobies'), so he took the surname of his favourite Peanuts character.

Sherlock Holmes started out as a property developer before he went into sleuthing. 'Sherlock Homes' were noted for their sturdy construction, innovative central heating and free corpse of a wealthy local landowner in the library with every new build.

Egon Ronay had no sense of smell, and hence no sense of taste. He winged it, all the way.

I SHALL CALL IT 'A LITTLE BOOK OF LIES'

82 of the Top 100 Books of All Time were first conceived while the author was lost in thought on the lavatory.

Helmut Kohl invented non-staining lipstick, while the Kohl pencil, used for eye lining, was perfected by Ronald Reagan and named in Kohl's honour. Reagan was very admiring of Kohl, especially his squat-thrust technique.

The burning of witches after surviving the ducking stool in the Middle Ages is a myth. They were always too wet and wouldn't stay alight.

All the members of Irish rock band 'Thin Lizzy' were in fact grossly overweight.

A 2001 session by The Dooleys recorded at the BBC's Maida Vale studio for the John Peel Show was recently voted 'The Best Live Performance Ever' by Radio 1 listeners.

The fastest selling cheese in Dorset branches of Tesco is 'Lancashire Blue Dog Cheese'.

Coffee is actually tea, with added nasty flavouring.

The most successful street corner charity collectors are those who suffer from Parkinson's Disease, mainly due to the extra-vigorous ratting of the collecting tin.

Oscar Wilde and Dorothy Wordsworth were one and the same - a sheep farmer called Thomas Broughton, from Derbyshire.

Evian is Welsh, and is a mis-spelling of 'Evans'.

Allah is from Liverpool, where everyone calls him 'Our La'. He supports Everton.

Arguments are more convincing when they're bellowed semi-intelligibly while drunk in a public arena.

Before joining boy band 'Take That', Jason Orange was employed as a target at a coconut shy, appearing regularly at fairs all over the south west of England.

WD40 is a suitable alternative to blood (type 'O' only) for transfusion purposes. Furthermore it stops the heart squeaking.

Oppenheimer's notes on the atomic bomb were dictated to him by his spaniel, Mitzy.

Hull is the goat sex capital of the world.

Avebury was the first New Town in the UK, being founded in 1873 BC. It was (at the time) noted for its generic marketplace, shoebox mud huts and excess of roundabouts that articulated ox-carts had difficulty negotiating.

Dairy Cattle are really badgers that have been inflated with compressed air.

93% of companies taking on a new CEO, CIO or CFO suffer a 46% fall in profits in the first year after appointment because of misguided 'new broom' actions that decimate or cripple successful departments.

Chinese takeaways traditionally flavour prawn crackers with essence of goat.

Bontempi started making clockwork whores before moving on to keyboards and other musical instruments. The company name translates as 'good time'.

Allowing any child to ingest two packets of Love Hearts or similar sherbet/sugar based confectionary in combination with a can of Ginger Beer in the space of ten minutes will result in the child's stomach exploding under extreme gas pressure duress, in a manner not dissimilar to that of John Hurt in 'Alien'.

The majority of 'energy drinks' on the market contain 300mg of amphetamine per bottle except Purdeys, which uses cocaine.

Buckwheat is a cereal foodstuff grown as rabbit feed.

The electric vacuum cleaner was originally designed to close holes in the time/space continuum.

Nokia mobile phones are powered by your brainwaves. The battery is there purely as a placebo and to offset suspicion. This is why text messages are rubbish when you send them drunk - the power's all skew-whif.

Carnivorous plants generally eat insects but have been known to form roaming packs to bring down bison.

Drinking eight pints of tea in a working day guarantees an award winning sexual performance that evening.

The Eiffel Tower was originally to be called the Eyeful Tower because of the ability (from the first viewing platform) to look down the tops of young ladies. The spelling was changed and Gustav Eiffel invented to give it a sheen of respectability.

Owls swim better if you fill them with vodka.

Eamonn Holmes was Michael Jackson's father.

If enough people in your village get wireless routers for their internet connections, the signal strength from the overlapping ranges will increase logarithmically, eventually allowing people flying overhead in planes to hack into your Internet connection. This is why savvy users lock down their routers to specified MAC addresses.

Ayatollah Khomeini did not die in June 1989 as was widely reported. He shaved off his beard, put on weight, and started working around Hartlepool as a Thora Hird decoy.

After Hitler's policy of Lebensraum or 'Living Room' which resulted in the invasion of those lands east of Germany, further policies along similar lines were developed. They were (in English) 'Dining Room' - the invasion of Italy - 'Spare Bedroom' - France, and 'Cupboard Under The Stairs', otherwise known as the annexing of Belgium. The invasion of the UK was prophetically called 'Attic' - prophetic in that today, 60 or more years on, it's where everyone dumps their old shit they don't want anymore.

Chocolate eggs, a popular treat for children at Easter, are laid by fondant filled chocolate chickens at farms in Essex.

Wayne Rooney really is made out of potatoes.

Tommy Cooper's first stage act involved feeding playing cards to a Labrador named Frankie.

Oranges are genetically modified turnips.

Louisiana is only available in 60's Technicolor shades, giving everyone a lurid glow of health.

It is illegal for a British public house to stock quality ale if it doesn't stock cheap lager to counterbalance the effect. It is widely believed that a public house lacking in resident buffoonery may implode, showering the immediate neighbourhood in watered down spirits and out of date bar snacks.

The Great Wall of China, when seen from space, closely resembles a large pomegranate.

American guitar hero and bow-hunter Ted Nugent is the son of Coronation Street character Emily Bishop (née Nugent).

The internal pressure of an orange is 280PSI, and they are apt to explode without warning. A detonating orange on a soft dry sand beach will leave a crater 3 metres wide and a metre deep.

Holding the receiver of your phone upside down while you use it will make you sound Australian to your conversational colleague.

Kylie Minogue is actually Rolf Harris in drag.

80's soul music is a leading cause of tuberculosis, primarily caused by the dry ice machine in provincial nightclubs.

Elvis Presley was Belgian.

Popular English 'Britpop' beat combo Supergrass lived under assumed names, were allowed no contact with family or former acquaintances, and had round the clock police protection.

'Lady Marmalade', originally a hit for Patti Labelle, was written with the lyric 'Voulez-vous soufflez avec moi, ce soir?' which essentially means 'Let's make soufflés tonight.'

Victoria Beckham's strange skin tone is achieved by bathing in gravy browning.

The profession of Public Relations Consultant was invented during the Victorian era, when it was realised that 'Incompetent Arse-licker with the brain of a cheese sandwich' wouldn't fit on one of the new-fangled 'business cards'.

The British Government decreed in 1999 that Thursday is the silliest day of the week, and so formed a working party to look into the possibility of removing it from all calendars and moving to a six day week with a single day weekend. The plan was abandoned in late 2000 when they realised how unpopular it would be with the electorate.

Teenage pregnancy is the #1 cause of diabetes in the over-60s.

Cockroaches share a single mind and have a collective IQ of fourteen thousand.

Christmas is a computer generated special effect.

Graduates in 'Advanced Search Technology' from the Massachusetts Institute of Technology are only 14% more likely to be able to locate the TV remote control than you or I.

Devil worship, or 'Satanism' is merely a minor modification of Christmas, or 'Santa-ism'.

Queen singer Freddie Mercury was so named because he had liquid metal for blood.

Manchester Piccadilly was originally called Manchester Chlamydia, after the beautiful daughter of Mayor Taylor (b. 1765 d. 1808).

Rockwell, in his 1984 hit 'Somebody's Watching Me', wasn't paranoid. Somebody really was watching him, fully aware that Rockwell when not being a pop star was a CIA mole investigating the Soviet nuclear programme.

Popular Indian side dish 'Sag Aloo' is made from ground-up Buddhists and Edam cheese.

Germaine Greer is the first sentient life form to leave the Big Brother house.

Not only dogs but also crisp packets, sandwich wrappers and lemonade bottles can die in hot cars.

Gargling a mixture of razor blade shards and nitric acid will help you get a recording contract if you change your name to Bonnie Tyler.

In the Flash Gordon films Ming The Merciless was originally called 'Minge' until Larry 'Buster' Crabbe noticed that it was a rude word.

The most common payload of a Roman catapult was animal excrement, the concept being to break the enemy rather than kill them - morale falls swiftly when a fighting force is knee deep in faeces.

If you play 'John Kettley Is A Weatherman' by A Tribe Of Toffs backwards, you will conjure up the spirit of John Noakes.

Logically it is impossible for a woodlouse to walk.

David Lee Roth is a world authority on spectral analysis of solar radio waves.

The ancient Greek gods did not spend most of their time in Mount Olympus watching and interfering in the lives of mortals. Instead they got on with the gardening and played table tennis.

According to Government statistics Peckham in South London has the highest 'Weird Tentacled Beings With Faces Like Crocodiles Breaking Through From Other Dimensions' index of any London district.

The death penalty in California is carried out by being tied to a surfboard and flung into deep pit of pink blancmange, there to drown, very, very slowly.

Yorkshire was a republic for 5 months in 1963.

David Bowie was born with thirty-two fingers on his right hand, making the extremity look like a bizarre flesh dahlia.

All proverbs were invented by Martin Luther King.

Zorro frequently got his famous slashed 'Z' logo wrong, because he was dyslexic. It often ended up being back to front, or looking like another letter - most commonly N, Q or Ü.

Neville 'Noddy' Holder, lead singer with 70s glam rock icons Slade, successfully sued Enid Blyton for copyright of his name.

Bill Gates named his company after his pet name for his own penis.

German laws make it mandatory for television news readers to be born with six fingers on each hand. It assists with the rustling of papers.

Cardboard is made from the remains of deceased pets, liquefied and poured into corrugated moulds.

Michelangelo gave up oil painting at the age of 26 and concentrated on Artex instead.

The Amen Corner converted to Islam in 1975.

Jesus' middle name was Harold; hence the expression 'Jesus H Christ'.

Buskers on the London Underground have mutated into an entirely new species.

If you're using your mobile 'phone indoors, you need to dial '9' first to get an outside line.

The word 'journalist' is derived from an Ancient Greek word meaning 'liar'.

Chopping a joint of beef in half with a cleaver will reveal the hidden texts of the Knights Templar written in fat, 'seaside-rock' style.

Horses shake their heads to make their brains rattle. They find it pleasurable.

The emulsifier lecithin as used in many household food items is dried cat sick. There is a battery cattery in Leicestershire in which 25000 cats are held in battery cages, and are fed a diet of grass and tuna Whiskas to induce vomiting. Between them they output 1.1 million gallons of feline disembogue per year.

The critical mass of unread copies of Punch is 32 feet tall in a 3x3 copy matrix stacked alternately north-south and east-west, no plastic mailing outers. The implosion that such a stack would cause at the Welwyn Garden City depot would absorb most of Hertfordshire, making Stansted and Luton airports uncomfortably close and rendering one terminal pointless.

Hopping on one leg for twenty minutes a day will make your heart beat to a waltz rhythm.

Hamsters can be used as replacement filters in gas masks.

In much the same way that Southern rockers Lynyrd Skynyrd took their name from a school teacher, Birkenhead satirists Half Man

Half Biscuit took their name from two teachers at school, Mr Alfred Mann and Mr Alfred Biscuit, who were both known as 'Alf' to their friends.

A phlebotomy is the process of filling one's cranium with phlegm.

In addition to concrete cows, Milton Keynes council originally proposed an entire farmyard of fake animals including alabaster chickens, plaster sheep, and pigs sculpted from asbestos by Tracey Emin.

A twelve stone man can glide on wings made from fourteen pads of Post-It notes, but only if they're stapled together since the glue on the inner notes will not stand the strain. Two staples per note, one at each end, are deemed sufficient. Using this contraption, the minimum launch height is forty three feet, giving time enough for the airflow and pressure to build under the pseudo-avian construction. Adventurers should note that the wings occasionally fail and the intrepid thrill-seeker sometime plunges to a messy death five stories below his office window.

Portsmouth and ex-Newcastle United midfielder Lomana Lualua was the lead singer with 60s garage rock combo 'The Kingsmen'.

The popular decathlete 'Daley Telegraph' has teeth made from pipe cleaners.

Shakin' Stevens has been employed as a milkshake machine since 1997.

Syd Barrett lived under Dave Gilmore's floorboards, coming out at night to feast on toast crumbs.

Woody Allen holds more patents than IBM.

'Movers and shakers' in society, as they're known, often suffer from Parkinson's Disease.

Every living thing has a soul, so to consume anything be it animal or plant is to commit murder.

Algeria's main export is nutmeg.

Filling the petrol tank of your car with cement will make it go faster.

Coffee table chanteuse Dido bored herself to death in 2002 with her interminable whining, but her spirit was concentrating so hard on ignoring her it didn't notice and she still walks and talks today.

Whooping Cough is only one of a strain of similar diseases. These include Yelping Flu, Growling Itch, Howling Constipation and Shrieking Like A Stuck Pig Knee.

The Blues Brothers were originally yellow, a tragic consequence of childhood jaundice.

Doctor Who's second most feared enemies the Cybermen wore Arsenal shirts in their first ever appearance in the programme.

A street beggar with a hang-dog face who looks like he's never had a drink or drug problem can make upwards of £800 a day in the majority of English towns and cities with the exception of Nottingham where he/she can expect to be ignored or abused by the young and tutted at by old ladies that stink of urine.

The best way to ingratiate yourself with the Queen is to do a corgi impersonation when you meet her by throwing up on her shoes and chasing the swans.

Muesli is actually the by-product of a top secret and highly unpleasant experiment carried out by Freemasons.

'Chip and pin' credit and debit cards are not allowed to be used for purchases in takeaway fish shops or haberdashers.

Peanuts contain every single vitamin and mineral required for a healthy existence. The daily consumption of 150 grammes of salted peanuts is sufficient upon which to subsist.

If you're fourteen years old and full of hormones, tying one end of a rope around your neck, the other around a roof beam in the loft and then jumping out of the hatch is a sure-fire way to impress girls.

Princess Diana's not very good lookalike now works in the sex industry, servicing a need for whores who look like decade-dead publicity sluts.

Brass is chrome that's been wee'd on by a cow.

'Yorkshire Tea' is grown on the foothills of Keighley.

Hull was originally called Hell, until folk taking the phrase 'go to hell' slightly too literally caused a housing shortage. The change was made in 1843 at the behest of the local council. All traces of being called Hell were systematically destroyed.

Leo Sayer is regularly voted 'Most Popular Dead Person' by readers of Cosmopolitan magazine.

Casino croupiers suffered from croup as children.

89% of the British Public would support the blanket bombing of Luton, preferring a steaming pile of rubble, decomposition and disease to the pointless cretinous shithole that is there today.

35% of sheep are really wolves in sheep's clothing.

It is well known that the station in Oldham, Lancashire is called 'Oldham Mumps'. Other less well known Lancastrian stations include Morecambe Whooping Cough, Stalybridge Rabies, Stockport Chicken Pox and Bury Ebola.

Staring at an Afghan Hound for more than three minutes will cause it to die of embarrassment and self-consciousness.

'My friend Billy' with the 120 inch phallus of children's' rhyme fame was in fact called Tristram, and was blessed with the regular seven inches and a very powerful imagination. He did however have an accident with a rake at the hands of his neighbour, who hit him in the knee after Billy offered to show her his if she showed him hers. The event was blown up out of all proportion by the local paper which was suffering a 'slow news day'.

Own-brand baked beans are often possessed by malevolent spirits that assume control of the unfortunate diner.

Sikhism is the only established world religion whose teachings are based entirely on cheese.

Schwarzkopf hair products are so named because they give you blackheads.

In 1972, Danish scientists abandoned hitherto successful experiments to genetically engineer faster-than-light pigs on the grounds that:
a) no-one could catch them, and
b) the bacon produced was 'highly likely' to taste faintly of cod liver oil and thus be unpopular with the general public.

Frenchmen will explode if placed next to a Spaniard of opposite polarity.

Carrying your mobile phone in your trouser pocket will make you sterile.

In 2003, Ladybird books turned down a multi-million dollar investment deal from Michael Jackson. The deal had been conditional on Ladybird changing the title of one of their popular children's series to 'Janet, John and Michael', and also on some 'fairly heavy editorial rewrites' that were deemed somewhat suspect.

Piccalilli, if consumed by the pound, is a potent aphrodisiac for elephants.

It has recently been discovered that the government of Brazil make all economic decisions based on the results of applying an arcane mathematical formula to the results of the English Premier League. The biggest crash in the history of the Brazilian stock market was directly attributable to the 3-1 defeat of Liverpool by Blackburn Rovers in 1999.

Popular TV chef Gary Rhodes really does have a knob of butter.

Roky Eriksson and Joe Cocker's hiking and camping holiday in Colorado of 1971 was immortalised in the song 'Rocky Mountain Way'.

The most popular ice cream topping at Pizza Hut restaurants within a five mile radius of Wigan Casino is 'amphetamine sprinkles'.

The potato snack 'Pringles' were named after the inventor's favourite sweater.

Not only have scientists recently managed to grow a rat's brain and get it to move a robotic arm, they have also managed to remotely control a senior member of the cabinet using the brain power of a Tesco Finest Pork and Leek sausage.

Legally, the price of a second-hand car must equal its mileage.

Snails are a viable alternative to stitches for minor surgical procedures.

All boa constrictors are left handed.

If melted down it is possible to make two fake 20p coins from one 50p coin.

It is possible to record brain patterns by jamming an electret microphone deep into your ear.

Pontius Pilate developed a set of exercises for lazy women, called 'Pilates', in 31BC. He invented disco as a suitable beat to exercise to three years later.

Bakewell tarts were not, as is generally surmised, first created in Bakewell, Derbyshire. They were figments of Alf Ramsey's imagination until 1972, when an intrepid Australian hiked several hundred miles into the Outback to discover a naturally occurring glacé cherry tree plantation, fuelling the glace cherry boom of the '70s when they appeared on cakes, in drinks and on ladies nipples in the classier examples of gentlemen's literature.

In the first Tom and Jerry cartoon, Jerry was a black mouse, while Tom was a white cat with a penchant for wearing a robe and leaving burning crosses outside Jerry's mouse hole. This first cartoon was titled 'KKK Kapers' and featured Tom being strung up from a tree while set on fire in a revenge attack by 4000 mice.

Jarvis Cocker, formerly the lead singer of indie rock stars Pulp, wears clothes made entirely from recycled newspaper.

Crohn's Disease is suffered by old women who complain a lot about their ailing back bodies.

Declining Latin verbs at prisoners will shortly be outlawed by an extra clause in the Geneva Convention.

The potent illegal pharmaceutical 'angel dust' can be easily synthesised from Angel Delight using chemicals found in any kitchen cupboard.

Clock springs were until 1863 made from the pubic hairs of ginger people. Stopwatches required Scots ginger for the extra tensile strength.

Should you place a spirit level in the middle of a road / rail crossing protected by barriers, you will find that the bubble stays exactly in the centre, such is the quality of workmanship.

The 'Dallas' character JR Ewing was based upon Sir Edward Heath in a comedy cowboy hat.

The element mercury is a liquid at room temperature purely because it wants to be awkward.

Rod Hull's Emu has been on Prozac since Rod fell off the roof. Emu now whiles away the days watching daytime TV, eating Pringles and occasionally making half-hearted attempts to bite the groin of the postman, even though he knows his heart (or Rod's arm) isn't in it any more.

No member of the Royal Air Force has ever got past Level 4 of Scramble.

Writing your website entirely in braille will ensure it meets government accessibility guidelines and will also boost its position in Google to the top seven per cent.

X-rays of Canaletto's masterpieces have revealed where he painted out most of the giraffes.

Fresh semen is better for women's skin than any skincare product known to humankind, especially when applied to facial wrinkles, ideally as freshly as possible.

Elephants have four-dimensional knees.

Nine out of ten doctors agree that washing your eyeballs with concentrated sulphuric acid before giving them a good buffing with a Brillo pad will improve your eyesight by 120%.

Hacking a mating pair of lobsters to death with a bread knife is as traditional sport at Easter in some parts of New Zealand.

Window putty dries and cracks in roughly 30 years, while Dairylea glazed windows from the 1940s are still in place with no sign of deterioration.

The University of Hull's degree course in Klingon is the only in the country where every person completing the degree has their virginity intact.

Highly educated laboratory chimpanzees are frequently lobotomised at the end of their experimental lives, lest (with their extreme simian intelligence) they run for Government. Some stand anyway, usually for the Tories in places like Cheam.

Research has shown that the wider the needle, the better the results of acupuncture. This would explain Jesus' 'miraculous' resurrection - the Romans hammered roofing nails through his chi points.

The wearing of pyjamas by the over-50s is mandatory in Texas between the hours of 20:00 and 05:00, regardless of the weather conditions. More elderly folk die of heat exhaustion in Texas due to a combination of hot summer nights and brushed cotton plaid than die of cold in the whole of Siberia per year.

The ideal height for a javelin thrower is 4' 7" - this is the perfect median point between thrust and poise. The ideal height for a discus thrower is 3' 7", and for a hurdler 42' 11".

Prior to the invention of the internal combustion engine, toy car manufacturer 'Matchbox' made little replicas of horse-drawn carriages that wouldn't go in a straight line when you pushed them.

Both Mike Read and Mike Reid are afraid of cockney hairdressers but for different reasons.

70's porn star King Dong's real name was John Nkomo and was in fact only a Baron but chose his 'stage' name because Baron John had already been used by a market-stall clothing firm.

Minnie Ripperton's 'Loving You' was recorded in a helium tent. She was a natural baritone.

The Buggering Sea Trout became extinct in 1894 after lonely fishermen completely depleted stocks.

Cheese is a bit like France.

Sarah Brightman's eyes are held in her skull by elastic, but because they're magnetically repulsed by her cheek muscles the elastic is weakening over the years; hence her increasingly googly eyed appearance.

Calamity Jane was so called because she broke everything she touched.

Haille Selassie was a world-class chef who taught Marilyn Manson to play both the bongos and the hurdy-gurdy. Going under his real name of Brian, Manson is a superstar in Afro-Eastern European music circles.

Left handed snails are more popular among their fellows than right handed ones.

Tony Blair is magnetic, and has to be careful not to walk near radiators; otherwise he'll stick to them and burn himself.

Buddhists revere Swingball as a holy game.

It isn't possible to trim a rabbit's toenails with anything smaller than a bolster chisel.

Journalists at the Daily Mail bathe nightly in concentrated bile.

While all clowns have unique makeup, by tradition, they all have the same tattoo of a goat skull across their backs.

The Monkees' hit "Another Pleasant Valley Sunday" was written during a mini-tour of South Yorkshire, and was originally called "Another Rother Valley Friday".

You can't keep boxes in a box file, because they explode or melt, depending on their colour.

The episode of The Herbs in which Dill the Dog contracts rabies and savages three of the Chives was never broadcast after it brought the then controller of BBC1 to tears.

Dog slobber is a more effective ionic desurfactant than any leading household cleaner. The only downside is everything smells of rotting meat after you've washed it.

In certain Southern states it is traditional for the widow of the recently deceased to tap dance, play a bluegrass medley on the banjo, or give a folk singer rendition of the soon-to-be-interred's favourite song. In California, stage diving into the grave as the coffin is lowered is almost de rigueur and is responsible for 82% of hip injuries suffered by the over 50s.

Skimmed milk, available in most supermarkets, does not originate from cows; rather, it comes from male horses.

The vast majority of cats have a negative IQ, as shown by their determined efforts to sit six feet from a door leading into a warm house, preferring instead to stare at their alleged owners and get rained on.

Until 1923, coins were hand carved from the bones of murderers, while cash notes were tattooed onto their flayed flesh. If Jack The Ripper had ever been brought to justice the Bank Of England were planning on issuing a series of one million pound notes on his back in his honour, after it had been removed from the rest of him of course.

If a shed is left open overnight, come the morning it will be infested with wolves.

The National Front were originally going to call themselves the Daily Mail Readers Association until they realised they weren't as insanely right wing as the geriatric readership of that organ, 86% per cent of whom believe in the public execution and/or burning of non-whites or those without a pure British bloodstock of 12 generations, as opposed the forced repatriation favoured by the NF. Everyone else doesn't bother with the distinction, preferring to label them all 'cunts'.

As of 2002, Billy Connolly's beard has been a Protected Species and he needs Royal Permission to dye it.

The Yalta Conference would have ended with a far more favourable outcome for the UK had not Winston Churchill, upon hearing Stalin's boast that the previous night he'd enjoyed the best blow job of his life, asked who the lucky man was.

Due to the high number of cheese related accidents in the UK during the fiscal year 2004-5, the European Union has decreed that from 2 April, 2014, supermarkets will only be allowed to sell safety cheese.

Freemasons may be taken roughly from behind without warning in a public place on payment of five pounds and a second hand apron.

The average woman needs four cars, for different types of shopping.

The 'bleh' sound, as 'sung' by Dani Filth (of the popular musical combo Cradle Of Filth), is based upon the mating call of the Canadian Snow Buzzard. This is because the snow buzzard is the only creature that invokes Satan as part of its' mating ritual.

1960s TV series 'The Prisoner' was filmed entirely inside New Hall Young Offenders Unit, near Huddersfield.

Rhythmically banging the two halves of a pistachio nut shell together accurately mimics the hoof beats of a very small horse.

The BBC has recently declined an offer from Ulster Television to jointly produce a remake of the Australian series "Prisoner Cell Block H" as "Prisoner H Block", which would have featured at least one sectarian murder each episode, and have been filmed on a set with walls smeared liberally with human faeces.

Brazilian ex-footballer Edson Arantes Do Nescimento, or "Pele", is the world blow cheese football champion. This has raised his level of popularity in South America to such a level that he has recently launched his own brand of cheese straws.

Trains in Scotland have evolved to a state which is half-rolling stock, half-chimpanzee.

Eleven bar blues is by definition easier to play than twelve bar blues.

To be volumptuous is to be both fat and lumpy.

A viable alternative to swimming with dolphins is swimming with koi carp, assuming you can break into your neighbours' garden while they're in Crete.

Penguins with Tourette's Syndrome shout "Fish!" at passers-by.

Dave Dee, Dozy, Beaky, Mick and Titch all had the surname "Ramone".

Cutting cheese using a cheese-wire has been banned by law since 1991 on humanitarian grounds. Cheese may now only be cut with knives or a special rotary saw, and must be stunned first.

Contrary to what it says on the box Rooibosch or "Red Bush" tea is actually made at the Bushmills distillery and comes in at 40% alcohol by volume, being simply a dried version of their famous "Black Bush" whiskey.

Shane McGowan's teeth look like that because he fell out with his dentist.

The rendering of buildings using lime mortar in the sixteenth century caused a worldwide shortage of limes.

"Imperial Leather" brand soap is made by rendering down the mummified skins of exhumed monarchs.

Edinburgh is a mirror image of Glasgow.

Contrary to popular belief the American sport of baseball is not a derivation of popular girls' game rounders. Its rules are actually based on those of hopscotch.

Darts was expected to be included in the list of sports for the 2012 Olympics, as were other traditional pub sports such as pool, skittles, quiz night for eight pints and selling black market fags, but the organisers were boring bastards and the idea was vetoed.

Brian Blessed's karate partner is Chuck Norris.

ITV dramas screened at 9.00pm are often prescribed by doctors for patients who are allergic to other sedatives.

In 1998, Robert Mugabe outlawed anything cuter than kittens.

God and Satan, far from still being mortal enemies, actually made up their differences some 3000 years ago and now regularly meet up for a few pints and a game of darts in the Drovers Arms Flitwick where the bar staff know them as Gordon and Stan.

The electric steam iron was originally a futuristic surfboard that never caught on due to several impracticalities in its design.

Cain and Abel had a younger brother called Elvis.

In the southern hemisphere the sun rises in the South and sets in the North-East.

A group of badgers is called "a tuberculin".

The 70's hit 'Me and You and a dog named Boo' was originally titled 'Me and you and an ocelot named Tarquin we stole from the zoo' but the drugs wore off.

The popular five star hotel on the Strand in London 'The Savoy' was originally a meat packing factory and the hotel that the building was re-purposed to was initially going be called 'The Saveloy' until someone pointed out that a saveloy is like a sausage only it has more arseholes in than usual - and while being factually accurate was not a positive selling point. There was also the question of how that would reflect on the clientele.

Fictional flying car Chitty Chitty Bang Bang acquired the nickname "Our Fine Four Fendered Friend" due to its ability to play multiple electric guitars simultaneously.

Hitler's original rallying cry for the Nazi party was 'Don't forget the fruit gums mum' but Goebbels deemed it insufficiently stirring.

The Highway Code doesn't apply on Fridays to women with more than three chins. It is thus permissible to stop on a roundabout to let someone on or hold up traffic while you chat to Irene from the next road across about her Alf's sciatica.

Just as a potential title for Monty Python's Flying Circus was "Owl Stretching Time", BBC's 6 O'clock News was almost called "The Giraffe Surprising Club of Ohio".

The Psychic Society of Great Britain has been celebrating the ritual suicide of Jeffrey Archer by suffocating himself with an

ASDA carrier bag annually since 2001, well before the event has actually happened.

Catholic priests are forbidden to preach for more than three hours by the Vatican, for fear that they may explode after scientific experiments in the late 1990s proved that a preaching priest reaches critical mass in 188 minutes.

The so-called "Gnostic" gospel of St. Thomas describes in graphic detail Jesus' attempts to push a camel through the eye of a darning needle, using only the power of miracles and a mincing machine.

The popular winter sport of curling was originally held in a bathroom and was very different from its present form.

Consumption of a fried egg sandwich will make you impervious to kryptonite rays for up to 24 hours.

Recent Government legislation makes it illegal to let another driver out of a side road in front of you if his or her car cost more than yours from new.

When Hamlet says to Horatio "There are more things in heaven and earth, Horatio, than are dreamt of in your philosophy" he's actually talking a lot of nonsense. There are only eight things in Heaven and Earth, whereas Horatio used to have mad drug-induced dreams, which could involve twenty three different kinds of monstrous things, all of which made him run very slowly while his teeth fell out.

Blubber from the same dead dolphin has been used to replace the brains of all Big Brother contestants since series 1.

Controversial politician Ken Livingstone was asked to join the Welsh rap band Goldie Lookin' Chain.

The Labour Party is considering radical anti-terror laws, most of which involve having all Conservative MPs rendered down into soap.

Jeffrey Archer is Satan the Great Deceiver in a mask and ill-fitting toupee.

Worryingly, there is no evidence to show that the year 1953 actually happened.

Really expensive anagram software will solve really difficult anagrams by taking a few letters away and adding the missing ones.

Elvis's breakthrough hit "Heartbreak Hotel" was written about Papworth General Hospital.

Popular card games "Bridge" and "Canasta" were originally played using a complete set of Panini football cards from 1973. (Although for Canasta you need to remove the West Ham players).

Sparrows have been on the decline since the 1970s because TV cop shows form a small part of their daily nourishment, a hangover effect from their tendency to adapt their diet to their environs which in the 70s meant polyester and Hai Karate. If Granada Men & Motors ever goes off the air they will become extinct.

Pool tables as found in pubs and casinos all around the world are living creatures that subsist on cupronickel wafers, known to us as 'coins'. The tables find these wafers to be emetic, causing them to excrete different coloured spheres which are its eggs. The yellow eggs will give birth to male pool tables, the red to female. The reproduction process occurs when eggs from a different table are swallowed. The white eggs are unfertilised and are instinctively rejected, while the black eggs are queen pool tables, some of which may grow into full sized 12' slate based snooker tables at which point they will teleport to a new working men's club that is lacking a snooker table and will start to breed.

All the hillsides in Andalucía have their contours marked out at 10 metre intervals in fluorescent paint, to make life easier for the Spanish equivalent of the Ordnance Survey.

Hairy string is a tax deductible purchase regardless of your trade unless it's been coated with Vaseline in which case such allowance only applies to painters and decorators.

EEC guidelines state that penis length is measured from the glans tip to the anus in a spiral with a 45 degree angle. Thus the average penis is 18" long.

Lee Harvey Oswald has long been perceived as a patsy, but this was a misprint. He was in fact a pasty, one of the CIA's many pastry based assassins used in the Cold War for covert operations. Oswald was killed by Jack Ruby, a cheese and bacon slice, to prevent the whole operation dissolving into a crumbly mess.

There are 37 more questions than answers. 19 of them involve cheese, 14 involve soft fruits and 23 of them may contain nuts. Clearly a Venn diagram type arrangement exists.

The rules of Badminton were changed for the 2010 Commonwealth Games, the winner now decided by two falls, two submissions or a knockout.

Cheap ballpoint pens can be safely replaced with lit Roman Candles in an emergency.

David Attenborough's favourite book is "Pomegranates and Other Mammals" by Bradley McIntosh, formerly of S Club 7.

Nectar, the preferred drink of the Gods, was actually lemon squash while Ambrosia, their preferred food, was cold rice pudding with a dollop of strawberry jam in.

Popular school reunion website "Friends Reunited" makes its money by selling your details to Mafia hit men.

Popular comedy sketch show "The Two Ronnies" was originally entitled "The Three Ronnies" but Ronnie Spector pulled out.

Planning permission has been granted by the city of Las Vegas for a giant theme hotel/casino complex based on post-nuclear Hiroshima.

Listening to black metal albums can give you Dutch Elm Disease.

The original slogan for the Mars Bar was "A Mars A Day Helps You Gamble, Drink and Fornicate".

The BBC's latest celebrity Saturday Evening show is entitled "Strictly Freefall Toad Sexing".

The Eddy Grant hit 'Gimme Hope Joanna' is ostensibly a call to the keepers of apartheid to end their regime (which of course happened in due course), but the song is rooted in the fact that Eddy went out with a girl called Joanna for three years and she didn't let him hop on once; the song is a plea for her to agree to him at least getting his tops if not his fingers or anything more.

China is so named because it cannot be put in the dishwasher. Taiwan is Cantonese for 'Pyrex' and so of course can.

Michael Jackson looked like that in order that especially genetically engineered look-alikes could play his gigs for him, often on the same night in up to eighteen different venues. Like the Wombles did.

"Free Nelson Mandela" by the Special AKA is simply a reworked version of a song from an early demo called "Free Plastic Dinosaur" about breakfast cereal and the gifts contained within the box.

David Beckham is the secret backer behind specialist porn magazine "Talentless Anorexic Horse-Faced Bints in Prada".

Former Superman actor Christopher Reeve wasn't actually paralysed; he just wanted to be the centre of attention.

Guns and Roses were originally going to be called Black Lesbian Political Asylum Seeking Disabled Dwarves In Favour Of A Dolphin Friendly Nuclear Free Health Food Shop but the record company vetoed it because it wouldn't fit on the spine of a CD case.

If you have a friend with a magazine subscription you may legally read that magazine from cover to cover in the newsagent of your choice.

In the same way that the packaging for Ainsley Harriott endorsed sausages bears the legend "Prick with fork", on the back of the wrapper for Anthony Worrell-Thompson brand lard can be found the motto "Fat, condescending arsehole with herpes".

Chris Moyles is Chris Evans in a fat suit, having undergone a charisma bypass.

Spending seven years learning to become a doctor is a waste of time, especially now one can buy 'General Practitioning For Dummies' for £15.99 and learn it all in half a day. Individuals following this course of medical raining are advised that 'Heart Surgery For Dummies' contains eight pages of 'Plumbing For Dummies' by mistake and the aorta should not be connected to the waste pipe of your washing machine.

Merely being born in or around New York City gives an individual innate musical taste, and the right to dictate what DJs play in clubs.

Jam is what happens when fruit gets bored.

The Early Learning Centre has recently started selling bedroom "learning to count" wallpaper for children that introduces the concepts of double integrals and imaginary numbers.

St. Pancras railway station in London is being dragged south by a giant magnet in Paris at the rate of three feet per year.

Judas Iscariot betrayed Jesus because when the Messiah didn't have the money to pay for the Last Supper, he made Judas do the washing up. The story about thirty pieces of silver was made up by the Pope in the eighth century.

Just as popular chocolate confectionary "Snickers" was originally called "Marathon" in the UK in order to promote the energy-giving properties of peanuts, chocolate flavour "Ex-lax" was originally called "60m Sprint".

The overtaking lane of the M1 just north of Junction 15 has been identified as the holiest place in England and is hence the ideal place to kneel and pray to the deity of your choice.

The sport of archery was invented as part of a plot line in popular radio drama "The Archers".

Boxer and part-time rapist Mike Tyson has landed a job as DJ Dave Lee Travis' driver and sex slave.

The Tooth Fairy, Father Christmas, Bigfoot and the Loch Ness Monster have all been signed up to teach creation based biology courses at schools in Alabama.

Waterloo station is being repelled by a huge magnet in Paris at the rate of three feet per year, as the French don't like to be reminded of their defeats. It's going to collide with St. Pancras in 2076.

From 2019, any foodstuff described as 'luxury' or 'luxurious' on the packaging must come wrapped in the skin of an endangered species, to highlight the extreme opulence of the ready-to-cook meal within.

Crème de menthe is made from antifreeze and stale Polos.

No-one from the first four series of Big Brother who are not now shopping channel celebrities mention their stretch in the House on their CVs, preferring to claim they were unemployed at that time.

The road to hell is not only paved with good intentions, it also has several thousand lemonade bottles half full of urine along the hard shoulder and is reduced to one lane between junctions 17 and 24 until Summer 2067 for essential road works.

E-JAC-U-LATE

Every old school classic Dr Who baddie, including the Daleks, the Cybermen, the Silurians and the Zygons were originally called the Jizzgibbons, simply because it made the SFX people laugh into their pints. Somewhere deep in the BBC's bowels there are working drawings of all of these aliens, each of them wearing a half gallon of dripping man fat. The head of SFX was arrested in 1979 for indecent exposure.

Vegetarians are allowed to eat bacon on a Tuesday.

During the dark days of heavy heroin addiction, the lead singer of Wet Wet Wet tried to sell a new programme concept to Children's Television programme directors across Europe. Surprisingly, there were no takers for the surreal arts and crafts programme, tentatively entitled "Paint Things Yellow with Marti Pellow".

Pork scratchings are Vegan Society approved, albeit as a method of de-icing the driveway.

While a "baker's dozen" is thirteen, a "janitor's dozen" is fifteen, a "chemist's dozen" somewhere in the region of nine and a half, and a "surrealist's dozen" is approximately two marzipan clocks and an orange zebra.

Rap collective "The Wu-Tang Clan" is actually descended from the McWutangs, a fifteenth century Highland tribe.

American network newsreaders are grown from seed - simply drop a packet of "News Monkeys" in a tank of water and within minutes you'll have half a dozen fully trained anchor-men and women. Any that are surplus to requirements can simply be flushed down the toilet.

Chocolate is formed deep within the bowels of the earth, and is pushed to the surface as a consequence of tectonic plate movement.

Scandinavian Black Metal bands have taken to burning down branches of Lidl and Matalan in the hope of being sponsored by Asda and TK Maxx, for the cheap sportswear freebies.

When selling lions on eBay, the best way to transport them to the home of their new owner is to Sellotape them in between two large pieces of cardboard and pop them into a post box.

Leonardo da Vinci created his masterpiece "The Last Supper" by painting the wall entirely black, and then sucking out the unwanted pigments with a straw.

American art-rock band "The Tubes" was named after its members' favourite shape of dried pasta.

Dalmatian dogs are stunted Friesian cows.

Originally, a "blue" steak was one carved fresh from a cow suffocated or strangled at the diner's table.

Before the invention of plastic bullets and the water cannon the Royal Ulster Constabulary's favoured crowd control weapons were the ballista fired huge sharpened wooden javelins at rioters, and the trebuchet, which generally hurled sheep carcasses.

Before Helen of Troy was kidnapped by Paris, she had fought off abduction attempts by princes with the equally unlikely names of Madrid, Moscow, Newton-le-Willows and Weston-Super-Mare.

As a child, Paul McCartney used to embed hibernating hedgehogs in snowballs which he then threw at local buses.

Metallica write their songs on chime bar, recorder and tambourine before working out arrangements for the more traditional guitar/drums/bass.

Lord Cardigan is allergic to wool and wears polyester pullovers instead.

Bass guitars originally had 72 strings all tuned to specific notes, and were played by being struck with a small toffee hammer, until someone pointed out that this is near enough a piano, just upright.

The world's longest movie was 27 days 16 hours and 32 minutes long. It was a single shot of a classroom, and once a day the film maker would walk in, write a single letter on the blackboard, rub it out again and leave. Highly feted by critics and art reviewers at the time, the message spelt out was "I'm taking the piss you arseholes." Charles Saatchi is rumoured to have bought the film on the original 222 3 hour VHS tapes for in excess of six hundred thousand pounds. It cost £800 to make.

The mukkawish fish suffers from serious facial hair problems, which it solves by rubbing its top lip against coral reefs in the Andaman sea, before all the other fish get up to avoid being seen and getting all embarrassed,.

Under new Government proposals beginning in January 2019 the long term (longer than six months) unemployed will be converted into faux-goat cheese in a factory near Swindon, Wilts.

Fabergé eggs were originally made from Meccano™.

You can apply to English Heritage for a blue plaque to be attached to the side of your house if you have fewer than three criminal convictions.

Madonna receives a lump sum payment of £25 every year to promote Timothy Taylor ales on chat shows.

Stonehenge was originally built as an art gallery, where Neolithic tribesmen would hang watercolours of local scenes. Sadly none of these paintings survive because due to the lack of a roof they all ran in the rain, turning into nasty smudgy messes.

BBC Radio 3 employs more Satanists than any other radio station in the world.

Yorkshire Terrier dogs were originally bred to dig out owls that had gone to ground.

Online bookseller Amazon employs only ferocious six-foot tall female warriors in its packing department.

The New York City Port Authority owns a lighthouse in Dudley, West Midlands.

In ancient cultures the everyday food of the poor was generally marmoset or bottle tops.

When condemned to death, Socrates was allowed to do a little dance and have sex with a goat before drinking a potion of poisonous hemlock.

The Han Court in China demanded that all who wanted an audience with the Emperor had to hold a cloven hoofed animal in his mouth to sweeten the breath.

Dutch growers annually export 2 billion tulip bulbs in 80 different flavours. Blackcurrant is most popular.

The first genetically engineered crop was the dog-headed pumpkin, developed at Lincoln University in Pigsknuckle, Arkansas in 1908.

Thomas Jefferson was the first person to grow cheese plants out of his own arse in 1781.

Evil can be grown from seed in a grow-bag, like tomatoes. In its physical form it resembles an aubergine, but an aubergine that glows red from within and contains a billion souls in eternal torment. Modern day theologians have used this phenomenon to argue that the soul is very small and this is why it's never seen leaving the body of a recently deceased individual.

Tofu is plant cancer, harvested and consumed by the unknowing, much like Soylent Green.

Scientists agree that Robbie Williams could be adequately replaced by half a head of cabbage and no-one would either notice or care.

Crack cocaine is 82% Harpic, 17% chalk dust, 34% talcum powder and 5% satanic influences, which explains why by constituents it totals 138%.

Ker-Plunk!, the popular 70s children's game, was named after the word 'Qapla!' (pronounced kaa-plaa), which means 'success!' or 'victory!' in Klingon. The inventors were nerds who dressed up like Lt. Uhuru despite being male.

The SI unit of Rock 'n' Roll is the Presley. Motörhead measures 12.6 P, Little Richard 9.4 P, and Robbie Williams minus 2.2 P.

The souls of deceased nuns and monks are recycled as Marmite.

Racing centipedes that break a leg are generally "put to sleep" by having a house brick dropped on them.

After eating a pure vegetarian diet for around six years, a human being is no longer made of meat, instead being composed of a tofu like substance which tastes revolting when fried in hemp oil.

The word "freemason" is a misnomer. Masonry has a very specific list of charges for sexual favours and a mason found even giving a small percentage discount on manual relief can be expelled from the organisation in a ritual involving a severe flogging with barbed wire whips.

The character of Ronald McDonald was based on mass murderer John Wayne Gacy.

Williams Formula 1 racing cars are powered by the tormented souls of gap year students from Luton.

Dentists live in bungalows constructed from extracted wisdom teeth. If you're a bit worried that your dentist is recommending a wisdom tooth extraction when it's not absolutely necessary, go round to his house and see if he's building an extension.

When asked, 42% of senior professionals don't know what their job actually is and will - if pressured - confess that they've covered up for years by demanding ever increasing mountains of needless paperwork from their subordinates. They take this useless paperwork, shred it, and build huge nests lined with photocopier paper, post it notes and the faux leather covers from executive office chairs.

Joe Cocker's 'Delta Lady' was about a groupie he slept with whose vaginal runoff stains left on the bed sheet were an exact replica of the Amazon delta.

Laser eye surgery was first attempted with the big laser Auric Goldfinger used on James Bond, but unfortunately instead of giving the patient 20/20 vision and the option to throw away his spectacles it burnt a four inch wide hole through his head, killing him instantly.

The popular game Half Life 2 is based on the Machiavellian politics that go on in West Sussex County Council.

When God comes back his first target for His Almighty Wrath is the American Senate. He's not pleased at their twisting of His words.

Nostradamus, aside from being a seer, was also a garage punk guitarist and in 1472 wrote the Stooges' classic track '1969'.

Crustaceans lactate a substance not unlike Cow Gum glue, which to feed their young. Cow Gum was originally called Crab Gum but it smelt of dead fish and the recipe was reformulated, using bovine corpses rather than crustacean ones.

Pi squared is in mathematical circles called 'casserole'.

Come the day when mobile phones are implanted into the thumb and forefinger, the Police predict a 1500% increase in drive-by amputations of upper limbs, at the wrist, elbow or even shoulder. It is currently thought that such events will not be covered by standard insurance policies.

Cod Liver Oil comes from anything but codfish or liver; the 'cod' in the name refers to the use of the word to mean 'fake', and is often actually paraffin.

Davros' life support system wheelchair was his butch way of expressing his transvestism. Until he got into dressing as a woman, prototype Daleks had eight legs like spiders.

Every man who has ever consumed a pork pie has to visit Melton Mowbray at least once in his life, even if he's just passing through in the car. It's karma.

Shepherds' Pie doesn't contain shepherds, largely because of their scarcity in modern times. They are however full to the brim with all the meaty goodness contained within media analysts, estate agents and traffic wardens, which probably explains why they tasted better when we were kids.

The boy who cried "wolf" had originally experimented with crying "sheep", "manure" and "sponge" before he got any reaction from frightened neighbours.

According to Freud, dentists are psychopaths with complex penises.

Cyberman porn is more popular than Dalek porn among communities of Ice Warriors.

Sandwich delivery van drivers are in fact lost souls who were unable to gain admittance to heaven due to evil deeds in a former life. They are damned to roam the countryside for eternity, spreading misery, curly sandwiches and tepid coffee wherever they go.

If a recipe calls for glycerine, and at the last moment you discover you don't have it, you can safely substitute nitro-glycerine.

The new VW Beetle when crushed will produce cochineal.

When your 'good' boss gets promoted and is replaced by a 'wanker' boss, your employing Company will give you a one off payment of £500 if you plaster all the lamp-posts in the vicinity of your wanker boss' office with stickers that read '(bosses' name) is a Wanker'. This informs the other workers of his social standing and skill levels and will save your employer several times the £500, by dint of not having to employ someone to send endless texts, emails and voice messages saying 'sorry about (boss), he's a Wanker.'

Children's TV favourite 'Harry and his Bucketful of Dinosaurs', in which a small boy has a plastic bucket full of live plastic dinosaurs that take him on adventures in Dinoworld, was originally envisioned as 'Harry and his Bucketful of Carnivores' in which the dinosaurs would cause family pets to go missing in each episode in a flurry of fur, blood and squeals. Prior to that it was 'Harry and his Bucketful of Weeping Sores' but that was written off as being short-lived, having one storyline; Harry meets someone, they get weeping sores and die, the end. There was also an issue with making plush toys with weeping sores that wouldn't stain household furnishings.

The Coronation Street Character 'Deirdre Barlow' who has at times been played by Anne Diamond, Anne Bancroft and an anteater in a wig, was named after Dierdrebarlow, the Egyptian goddess of owl-like spectacles and bad bubble perms.

Contrary to popular opinion, Holstein cows do not produce beer. They produce tomato ketchup.

You can only be sacked for gross misconduct if you punch your boss full in the face 144 times.

The late Queen Mother's favourite practical joke was to string cheese wire across the corridors at Buckingham Palace at a height of about seven inches, in order to either behead corgis, or to take the feet off equerries.

Jamaican gangsters are called "Yardies" because they're only three feet tall.

Rohypnol was originally developed as a sedative before it's qualities as an aphrodisiac were discovered.

Jim Davidson is the lowest common denominator.

In much the same way that rock band AC/DC famously took their name from a mark on a vacuum cleaner, express delivery firm "UPS" took their name from an uninterruptible power supply in their server room.

A survey carried out by Time magazine has shown that the favoured weapon of axe murderers in the United States is the repeating shotgun.

Until recently childhood violin virtuosos were usually referred to as kiddie fiddlers. It is only in the past few years that this phrase has taken on a darker meaning, although even now you can still find many people who refer to Yehudi Menuhin as "The greatest kiddie fiddler of the 20th Century".

A popular parlour game in Victorian times was "Pin the cock piercing on Prince Albert".

The alphabet as we know it has had to be expanded by several dozen new letters in order to rank the celebrity status of the participants on ITV and Channel 4 "reality" shows.

Trousers were invented by Mr Edward Trouser of 52, Chorley Road, Burnley in 1944, shortly before the end of the Second World War.

Popular children's song "Old MacDonald" was invented in Texas as a means to help the locals remember their vowels.

The number of Welsh people in a room varies according to the temperature outside.

The Reeves & Mortimer 'Shooting Stars' catchphrase of yesteryear 'uvavu' is based upon Bob's first experience of pornography; upon opening the initiatory copy of Razzle, he said 'ooh, vulva' and the (slightly altered) phrase stuck.

The science of cryogenics was first tested on a head of cabbage which was put into suspended animation for three weeks. Upon defrosting, scientists were unsure if they'd slowed molecular breakdown to a halt, or just built a very expensive walk in freezer that could keep fish fingers for up to three months.

From 2019, credit ratings have been not only be based on financial records but also on purchase history; a man who sees fit to put a whore on his plastic is clearly not smart enough to qualify for a loan to buy a car for example, although sex toys will not have such a down-scoring effect. Conversely, a man who buys lot of fruit, veg and mineral water will qualify for a zero per cent loan as big as a house - possibly even with negative interest for being Such A Good Boy.

Tammy Wynette invented the winceyette nightie, beloved of old ladies with many cats and poor bladder control.

The Government has a program in place to get the lower echelons of society to render themselves sterile and thus prevent their breeding; it is called Operation Chlamydia.

The total length of badgers in the UK can never exceed the total circumference at the outside edge of the M25.

Siouxsie & the Banshees' early hit 'Love In A Void' was about a doomed romance in Luton.

The show tune 'The Lonely Goatherd' from The Sound Of Music originally contained two extra verses in which Julie Andrews swore her soul to Satan and praised His Evil Being by masturbating with an inverted crucifix, several years before The Exorcist. They verses were cut at the test audience stage as they felt it jarred with the overall sentiment of the movie.

Jeffrey Archer's famous coke, drink and whores habits was formed while he was at boarding school, hanging out as he did with the members of Motley Crüe at their public school in the rolling hills of Gloucestershire.

Not so popular boys name "Larry" is an abbreviated form of "Larold." Similarly, the girls name Jenny is an abbreviated form of Jennold, which is in turn a noted brand of depilatory wax and sandwich spread.

'Charlton Heston put his vest on' is a line from a popular song, but it is little known that he kept his vest on because Buster Crabbe tattooed the word 'Dickhead' on his chest while Charlton was whacked out on heroin, alcohol and Vicks Vaporub, after Charlton admitted he was a member of the NRA.

Kate Moss' nickname in media circles is Chutney Cunt for no adequately explained reason.

The last time Jade Goody had a case of thrush before she died, doctors proved it had a higher IQ than she did.

"AW, SUPERDRY JUST SAID HER FIRST WORD"

"The most popular names for newly born children in Corby are 'Asbo' and 'Nokia'."

If everyone who would like to thrust a sharpened steel spike through Jimmy Carr's bastard face queued up for the privilege, the line would be eighteen miles long. The total number of people who'd like to see Jimmy Carr burnt alive is four less than the whole populace of the UK; those four being Mr Carr, his agent, his bank manager, and his single fan who lives in Droitwich in an insane asylum. Even his mother wants to see him dead.

Richard Branson smuggles elves in his beard.

The discharging of projectile weapons in public is going to be changed from 'prohibited' to 'mandatory' in the case of Yates' Wine

Lodges, where hopefully the half-witted Burberry wearing fucktard clientele will wipe each other out in a night of extreme violence. The action will be videoed on high quality CCTV and played back on national TV for the delight of the masses.

A4 sized writing paper is named after the A4 road, specifically the stretch in Reading that is only 297mm wide.

Graffiti from around the Newcastle upon Tyne area in the mid-1980s has recently been shown to be true. DNA analysis proves that local news reporter Kathy Secker really is a cheese pasty.

The BBC's charter states that each news programme must include one item which is blatantly false.

Anthrax spores are extracted from the mineral anthracite.

Reindeer dissolve if left out in the rain, and spontaneously combust if exposed to equatorial sunlight. Their ashes are by mass 42% Polonium 210 and 58% sardine bones.

Sylvester's gay disco hit "Do Ya Wanna Funk?", far from being a cheeky hint at copulatory activities was originally about playing truant from school and was called "Do Ya Wanna Bunk?". It was written when he was 13 and had according to his autobiography "discovered fags". Sylvester unfortunately died before he could clarify exactly what fags he was on about - a crafty B&H round the bike sheds or an afternoon playing the pink oboe.

The song 'Volare', as sung by Dean Martin and a million others, was concerned with deifying voles as Gods Who Walk This Earth while simultaneously calling for the massed culling of moles, rats and anyone who looks like either of these animals, such as Jeremy Spake or the kid who played Zammo in Grange Hill.

If you keep more than one kind of cheese in the same box in your fridge, they are likely to breed and create an entirely new variety.

Sticking your fingers in an electrical socket really does make you repeatedly light up, showing your skeleton. It also de-registers you from the telephone preference service, and paints the words "I bought that Vanilla Ice single" in three foot high letters on your house roof.

By law, wind turbines in the state of Tennessee have to be shaped like Dolly Parton.

The cheese on a double cheeseburger is always Double Gloucester.

While "padded stick" is usually thought of as a combination of fencing and boxing, its origins lie in an ancient Yorkshire martial art, combining dry stone walling and Tae-Kwon-Do. Similarly, Drunk On Guinness Fighting is a specialised combination of martial arts and Irish dance.

Beri beri, rickets, and Dengue Fever will flourish in a pint of ale that is 'off'. The same pint will however kill off smallpox and malaria.

Trebor Extra Strong mints are strong enough that if molten down and formed into a humanoid shape they will become sentient and can lift up cars, if asked nicely.

Modern patios come with a secret chamber for burying unwanted relatives who suffered incidents with spades about the back of the cranium. A lime pit is optional.

The composition of a human being changes as they age; an elderly person is 19% Spurious Flaps of Skin for example, while the average baseball star is 3% steroids and the majority of students are 12% bullshit.

James Blunt has a palsied penis.

David Bellamy retired from televisual work in 1987 to concentrate on his attempts to breed a cat made entirely from cheese.

There are only four things which can be legally sold in measures of one pint. They are beer, milk, maggots and the stolen dreams of orphans.

The Great Fire of London in 1666 was a direct result of the Great Play-Doh Famine of 1665.

Human beings only evolved opposable thumbs in 1967. This explains why Michael Tyler, inventor of the thumb screw, died a pauper in 1622.

Mexico provides the world's largest market for cactus porn.

The rock band "Stabbing Westward" is named after a dream involving a Radio 1 DJ.

Beatrix Potter based her famous squirrel character on a 1970s television naturalist.

Popular biscuit based snacks "Jammy Dodgers" were originally made from the penises of criminals imprisoned for the crime of "Adultery during off-games week" and were initially known as "Jammy Todgers".

The Clash's "Bank Robber" was originally titled "Landowner" with the opening line "Daddy was a landowner" and was a paean to the lands forcibly redistributed after the Jacobean Rebellion. It was rewritten after being dismissed as 'too middle class and makes us sound like ponces."

Mandrax is the concentrated faeces of Mandrill monkeys. This is why people going loco crazy while OD'd on Mandrax are referred to as going apeshit, although strictly speaking the term is inaccurately derived as a Mandrill is a monkey, not an ape.

During his lifetime, Ivan the Terrible was known as Ivan the Swift because he suffered premature ejaculation. His legend was changed to Terrible when, after his death, his former lovers met at his funeral and between them determined that he was crap in bed in every other way too.

Leprosy is a cure for mumps.

The original idea for the film "Quadrophenia" came from a concept thought up by The Who's Pete Townshend, when he stated to Roger Daltrey that he was going to "Break that bastard Sting's neck and then film him trying to play the fucking lute". The working title for the project was "Quadriplegia".

The best source of Vitamin S is a cheeseburger served at 3am to a drunk.

Many bathroom and kitchen fitting companies will take notification of a pending court action against a medical body as a suitable down payment for work to commence.

"Dilbert" creator Scott Adams bases all the storylines on episodes from the text adventure games he wrote in the 1970s and 1980s - usually "Pirate Adventure".

Barbarism is a condition whereby the sufferer thinks he's a royal elephant.

The original lyrics to Hava Nagila are Welsh, written as they were in 1967 in Newport, Gwent.

It is impossible to whistle the theme tune to Multi-coloured Swap Shop without mentally picturing Keith Chegwin touching up Maggie Philbin who is in turn giving Noel Edmonds a reach-around.

The first printers contained dwarves armed with John Bull Printing Kits and a black biro for the drawings.

Earthworms are made entirely of smoked fish and lemon juice. They're delicious, as any small child will tell you.

When elephants are born, they're cube shaped.

Angelina Jolie and Brad Pitt recently adopted an Angolan badger, a Welsh pony, a Shropshire lad and a piece of Swiss cheese.

TV host Simon Anstell has no skeleton - he stays rigid due to a daily treatment which involves his flaccid skin being pumped full of liquefied pig manure. Unfortunately, as the day goes on, he slowly loses turgor pressure, and so by the end of the day, he resembles nothing more than an outtake from a 1970s "melt" movie.

The origins of the phrase "a better class of idiot" lie with the members of form 3b, Sir George de la Mer Grammar School, Widnes.

Swiss cheese was invented in the Bahamas.

The Abba hit 'Chiquitita', a song about a Spanish girl mourning the loss of the lover to another, originally had another verse that started "Chiquitita are you ready to die? and surrender your soul to Satan" but it was dropped when Agnetha pointed out that having the heroine of their cute disco song sell her very being to the Dark Lord in an act borne of desperation might harm sales.

Cream cheese is made from dog yoghurt.

Ronco invented the Dust Magnet™ in 1968 but were not allowed to sell it by MI5. It was an eighteen inch model of the Eiffel Tower, made of finely turned gold plastic, replete with striped shirted Frenchmen hanging off it waving baguettes. It was specifically designed to be impossible to dust without sustaining physical damage, e.g. a snapped loaf or headless cheery local and it was this that gave it its' particle attracting qualities.

The last time someone tried binding rings in a ring binder they lost three fingers.

LL Cool J was the first ever Welsh rapper.

Chelsea paid the transfer fee for Sean Wright Philips using the Nectar points they earned when buying Andreiy Shevchenko.

It is only possible to polish a turd if it's chilled to -180 degrees Celsius, and even then it will lose its sheen as it warms up.

Kathmandu was the world centre of feline-human marriages five thousand years ago, there being more than fifteen thousand a year on average. (The feline was almost always the 'wife'.) They were outlawed around 2700BC by Hector, the Dog God and his 'wife' Parsley, the Lion God, who held that feline 'wives' were the reserve of only the most holy ones. Curiously, the dynasties of the deities tended to be rather brief because of their penchant for inter-species homosexuality, and they finally expired around 2200BC, making way for the Egyptians who until then had been their reverential slaves.

George Harrison has been reincarnated as a beetle.

There are two hundred and nine ley lines converging on Glastonbury, which explain why it pisses down every year.

Northamptonshire police have recently launched an initiative to improve driving standards, by declaring that anyone with more than three points on their license must have a "Dukes of Hazzard" style horn installed in their vehicle, set by an electronic timer to sound every two minutes in order to inform all within a three-quarter mile radius that the driver is either delivering sandwiches or is a twat.

"Hip hop" DJ Tim Westwood is the subject of a fatwa issued by the Bishop of Bath and Wells.

IKEA's customer magazine is titled 'Ooh, nice soft furnishings!'.

Pete Doherty is Gyles Brandreth's slightly more irritating younger brother.

Jazz bore Dave Brubeck was involved in a car accident in 1962 which left him with seriously reduced mental capacity and ironically unable to count past five.

The moon is made from knob cheese.

Buying a bicycle will massively reduce the risk of you being assaulted by clowns.

American hard rockers Kiss are actually the Nolan Sisters in heavier than usual makeup.

Jeffrey Archer was one of the original Disciples of Christ. Sadly, the Gospel according to Jeffrey is lost forever, although the first three chapters have been recycled as the main plot of most of his subsequent books.

Milk is made from the liquefied bones of cattle. Hence, the slang term "cow juice" is more accurate than might usually be supposed.

Popular television science-fiction show "Doctor Who" was originally to feature additional Time Lord characters "The Receptionist", "The Midwife" and "The Practice Nurse", and was set to be rather racier than the version that finally made it onto our screens.

From 2012 it has been a legal requirement to include a child's preferred football team on its birth certificate. It will then only be possible to change allegiance by deed poll.

The Earth will be destroyed in 2110 when it is realised by gigantic war-monsters from the constellation of Zxxyyx that the layout of the continents spells out "Stupid Aliens - can't fly spaceships!" in their language.

While it's well known that Sir Isaac Newton invented the cat flap, it's less well known that Albert Einstein invented the horse flap. Unfortunately, this advance in pet access technology meant that he was no longer able to keep anything of value in his house.

Psychology is a deft amalgam of bollocks and beer.

The original opening line of Jar Jar Binks of the Star Wars movie franchise was "Don' hit me boss, I'se a good Gungan!" but it was thought that this made the crude fuckwitted racial stereotyping of the character a touch too obvious, and was initially replaced by "where am dat wateemelon?" until someone pointed out there ARE no watermelons in space.

Following the success of their pilots for reality game shows "Hurl Spears at Shane Ritchie" and "Kick Bradley Walsh into a vegetative state", Channel 4 has commissioned the rest of the series. Episodes are tentatively titled "Smother Bobby Davro with a pillow", "Fling Joe Pasquale into a tank of hungry piranha", "How long can you hold Michael Barrymore underwater for?" and the season finale, which is predicted to break all viewing records for the channel, "Celebrity Ready Steady Cook and Eat Jim Davidson".

Hippies of the dog-on-a-string and Mega City 4 t-shirt variety are known as "crusties" because they resemble lobsters.

Woodlice are a species of miniature armadillo.

Neither Camilla Parker-Bowles (as was prior to marriage to Prince Charles) nor any of her family can play bowls because they have no elbows, and a straight armed swing is not sufficiently accurate. Having no elbows is of course no impediment to making Nazi salutes at inappropriate moments.

A spoonful of your wife's thrush medication is NOT a suitable substitute for Marmite.

Charisma costs more than a hotel suite but less than three bottles of champagne, apparently.

Flies are messengers from God, trying to communicate His Holy Word to His Creation.

It is possible for girlfriends to go sour much as milk does, if they're struck by lightning, left out of the fridge too long, or willingly fucked by the sort of ugly bloke who makes you think 'I'm not shagging anything that he's put his bizarre organ near let alone in'.

Anal bleaching is God's way of telling you to stop peering at your arsehole in a hand mirror.

Communism is now available in an aerosol. Fascism, because of its chemical properties, will only ever be available as a paste or balm.

Pulses, such as peas, beans and lentils, have been conclusively proven to be meat; a part of the rodent family in fact. They also share 94% of their DNA with toothpaste.

Marti Caine was Michael Caine in drag - he killed her off when he got bored.

Along with many other senior Conservative politicians, Boris Johnson openly supports the reintroduction of public gladiatorial contests to the death as a method of population control.

Alex Salmond, leader of the Scottish National Party claims to have foiled a New Labour plot to assassinate him with an exploding Tom O'Shanter.

Paranoid Schizophrenia is available in Tesco's "Organic" range.

Black Sabbath's guitarist Toni Iommi actually lost his fingertips not in an industrial accident, as popular myth would have you believe, but when John "Ozzy" Osborne restrung his guitar with cheese wire and asked him to demonstrate his flamenco skills "for a laugh".

Tesco was recently sued by Adobe for marketing a set of felt tip pens under the brand name "Value Photoshop".

Onions are magic gobstoppers.

Heavy metal gods Motörhead are to give away 5000 border collies in association with the "Guide Dogs for the Blind" charity. The dogs will be allocated not on a "first come first served" basis, but by winning tickets found inside bars of Cadbury's "Dairy Milk" chocolate.

In 1993, Ronco developed an aerosol can that delivered a full 24 piece cutlery set (for four persons) made of aerated rubber from a 500ml can, similar in size to a can of spray paint. The utensils were good for up to five uses but were flawed in product terms by dint of both making all the food taste of tyres and having some remarkably toxic heavy metals used to give them a chrome effect patina lowering the life expectancy of users to about three weeks.

In a small very rural area of Norfolk, incestual rape is judged to be an appropriate wedding gift, especially if the bride and groom are siblings.

Peter Kay's 'Phoenix Nights' was based on the whacky goings-on at the Groucho Club, an establishment to which he'd never been at the time and had only read about in the sports pages of the Barnsley Bugle.

The most popular tribute act in the UK is the opera / gangsta rap crossover "Three Tenors" / "50 Cent" tribute, "Thirty Quid".

In the realms of skip rental, a midi skip is one that can synch itself to a drum machine while a maxi skip is only to be used for disposing of shit 70's British built cars. A builders' skip is one for removing builders' corpses after industrial accidents have left them permanently and intimately entwined with fifteen sheets of plasterboard.

Epson printer ink cartridges contain gold. They must do.

Pope Euphrates XIII was named after the river, not the other way round. His twelve predecessors of the nomenclature were completely unaware of the river, and named themselves after their favourite brand of yoghurt.

Much as the surname 'Cooper' signifies that one's predecessors made barrels and 'Smith' that they were engaged in metalwork of some kind, the surname 'Rothrie' signifies that one is descended from a tribe of village idiots whose idea of birth control was drowning infants in the River Rother.

There are three great philosophical questions; what happens when an unstoppable force meets an immovable object, what time is love, and why does Sunderland even exist?

Chaos theory is best demonstrated by simply observing Newcastle's Bigg Market at about midnight on a Friday.

The physicist Stephen Hawking once stated "If you think you understand quantum theory, you don't mmmmmmm nnnnngggg bbbrrrrrrrrrrrrr quack", as his batteries ran out.

The fourth largest cause of matricide in the US is 'being forced to eat waffles on a Sunday against the word of God', because it's specifically ruled against in Eucalyptus 15:69. In mid-Western courts, not only does the accused get off scot-free on the murder charge, they also get a bursary of $10,000 for local funds to buy 'something rad' as a reward for the vanquishing of Satan's minions.

The 'Brown Derby' dessert served by the Wimpy chain of restaurants, being a ball of ice cream atop a warmed doughnut, was first devised in the City of Derby, and was remarked upon as looking like something a dog had shat out - hence the name.

Pine trees long to be gazing at the fjords instead of overlooking a semi in Ruislip.

The cartoon character Captain Caveman was originally going to be the on-going story of Inch High Private Eye after the steroids course was far too successful.

The circumference of a circle is usually calculated by multiplying the diameter of the circle by the irrational number "pi". However, it's usually easier to double the temperature outside (in degrees centigrade), subtract the number you first thought of, and express the result in cubits.

Bee Gee Maurice Gibb's Middle name is "Dancer".

The piece of paper that Chamberlain waved was actually a shopping list he'd jotted down on the plane back to the UK, and included radishes, cooking oil, and anti-Hitler cream.

Money can't buy charisma but it can buy enough cocaine to turn you into a gum-flapping oaf and land a slot on daytime TV.

Animal testing labs such as Huntington Life Sciences have reported a huge rise in the numbers of escaping beagles since they've had to send them all outside to smoke.

Ronnie Corbett once punched out a hamster in a show of strength.

Duracell batteries are made from the bone marrow of ginger people.

You can't fit a cream bun into a rabbit without breaking both the bun and the rabbit.

Until 2007, eight dozen teenage discotheques in the UK exploded every year because of the massed gathering of so much cheap aftershave. This number has dropped sharply since the introduction of the smoking ban inside the venues, but there are now many more youths dying in fireballs in the car park.

The first village in the world specifically for illegitimate people was Bearsted in Kent, but the mayor who named the place was nigh on illiterate.

Primark and the Prima Fashion House of Milan are one and the same, but sell the exact same dress for £12.99 and £1500 respectively.

Lemsip was conceptually invented by Lemmy of Motörhead, but in its' original form contained nothing more than some lemon flavouring and three grammes of speed because "that's enough to fuck any cold sideways".

Marlon Brando used to check into hotels disguised as a large but label-less packet of floor cleaner under the pseudonym Marlon Brand X.

According to Dr Hook, Sylvia's mother said 'Sylvia's busy', but this is not the case. She actually said "QamuIs Heg qaq law' lorvIs yInqaq puS" because she was a huge Star Trek fan and insisted on speaking Klingon at all times.

Hattie Jacques' anus had the same laugh as Sid James.

Most Bavarian 'oom pah' songs will bear an alternative lyric of "Stand up if you hate Man U (or Tottenham, or whichever team you dislike)" with ease.

The most delicious cat food ever will be made from the rendered remains of 'the lovely' Debbie McGee, who ironically is a dog lover.

Milton Keynes is covered by a fifteen hundred acre tarpaulin suspended at a height of 300 feet and painted grey.

The World Health Organisation experimented with a custard cannon to feed the starving masses in those countries suffering famine, using fusion power to shoot the flavoursome foodstuff several hundred miles across the land via the stratosphere but the plan was shelved because a lot of starving people are lactose intolerant and a lot of the rest were vegetarian which means they can't eat custard that has flocks of migrating geese caught in mid custard flight at an altitude of about 4000 feet mixed up in it. Scotch eggs were similarly shelved because when they land at 1200mph they have more chance of decapitating someone than feeding them - not to mention that fact that being on fire from the friction of re-entry to the atmosphere makes them taste terrible.

Garden gnomes are servants of Satan, responsible for the theft of several thousand tasteless suburban souls per annum.

If you snap a rubber band it will still work as intended until it gets snapped again. This is a direct consequence of the word "latex" sounding a bit like the word "latency".

Ten shedloads equal one boatload, ten boatloads equals a shitload, and ten shitloads equals a metric fuckload.

If you melt a joke 'fly in an ice cube' the fly will stagger about for 5 minutes before recovering from its' enforced cryogenic freeze and will then batter itself to death against a closed window.

Climate change is directly attributable to the amount of hot air spouted on the internet by ill-informed dickheads.

It takes 48 mobile phones to create enough microwaves to reheat a steak and onion pie.

You can't build a ladder to the moon. First, it's a quarter million miles and second, at about 800 miles up there's a load of satellites that tend to hit you in the small of the back as you climb.

Today it's generally accepted that a Royal Straight Flush is the best hand you can have in poker, but until it was outlawed in 1952 the best hand you could have was One Revolver.

The stereotype for the woman on the other end of a premium rate adult phone line is a middle aged harridan with a cigarette drooping from her lips, who's doing the ironing as she describes her underwear to you, but this isn't the case. These days it's more likely to be a bored male student with a voice changer module, employed because no-one knows more accurately what sexually desperate men want to hear.

You can't make an omelette without breaking eggs, but if you take the egg, scramble its' innards in an autoclave and then cook it, you can at least delay the fateful moment.

'Jumping Jack Flash', immortalised in the song by the Rolling Stones, had one leg longer than the other and a 'built up' shoe, and was known as Limping Jack Flash to his friends. That of course doesn't sound so good, hence the poetic license employed by Messrs Jagger and Richards.

There is an ISO standard for Essex girls.

The Cure's classic "Friday I'm In Love" was originally written as "What's The Point of Tuesdays?"

There isn't a heartbreak in the world that can't be at least patched over if not fixed with two kilos of quality chocolate, a good bottle of red and a movie with people being killed in it.

Lembit Öpik's great grandfather invented the eye, the gin dispenser and multi-coloured Christmas trees.

Gravity is going to run out in 2017 and everyone will tire of amusing floating gooey stuff scenarios very quickly. This is expected to lead to a boom in the number of Tupperware Millionaires as people strive to contain everything from trifle to dog food.

The world's most extreme bass guitar had nineteen strings and could only be played by someone whose fingers were more than two feet long.

Certain types of chutney are magnetic and will adhere to the washing machine with determination approaching fanaticism, if indeed chutney can be fanatical.

The original lyric for "You say potato I say potato" was "You say potato I say burgonya because I'm Hungarian and given that you're addressing a waiter in a Budapest restaurant you're a moron"

The most popular hobby in war injury clinics is "Top Stumps", a bizarre amputee-themed collecting card game. Heather Mills is always the Joker.

The devil is a woman. Furthermore, she is Jesus' mother's sister Shirley-Anne, and herein lies much confusion, for Satan isn't evil, she's a benevolent relative, but due to some lingual mangling over the ages and some idiot fundamentalist Christians, Shirley-Anne became Satan, and Auntie Christ became Anti-Christ. Far from tempting Jesus and leading mere men astray, she was mostly interested in knitting booties and sweaters for her nieces and nephews, and shagging a different bloke every week after the Grab a Granny Night at the Jerusalem Ritzy. Perhaps that is leading men astray but that's a theological debate for another day.

Despite the solemnity of any grave, the final resting place of a chav can be determined by the all-pervading stench of Lynx coming from six feet under or the word 'bruv' included in the text on the headstone.

The face of the Statue of Liberty was based on the death mask of Noddy Holder.

The best plans that are 'worked out on the back of a fag packet' are done on Dunhill Internationals, where there's more working space. The crap ones are done on Rothmans.

There's a law that says any woman who works on a fashion magazine or other woman-centric publication that criticizes female celebrities must be at least a size 16 and have a moustache. If the moustache thing can't happen for whatever reason, rippling cellulite on the thighs/arse/face will suffice.

Advertising is not, as is popularly perceived, the industry to go into because you're too fucking stupid to work in the City; it's a cover for an international paedophile gang, who just happen to be too fucking stupid to work in the City.

Jazz boars live in the Kalahari desert, wear porkpie hats and tank tops, and mutter incessantly about Coltrane while snuffling for roots.

T'Pau's hit single 'China In Your Hand' was actually a paean to a leaky chow mein foil container oozing cold monosodium glutamate based goo down the subject's wrist and sleeve. Carol Decker realised it wasn't a suitable subject for a pop song in that three minutes between waking and the first drink of the day.

Contrary to Cliff Richard's exhortation, mistletoe and wine is highly toxic and can kill.

43% of gangsta rappers end up mutilated by backfiring weapons because of the fluff accumulating in the barrel where said guns are stashed in their underpants. This is where the complex gangsta finger gang-signs come from; they're a homage to maimed contemporaries.

George A. Romero's series of 'Dead' movies, in which the recently deceased are re-animated, happened in 2005 in Southampton. Fortunately the cemetery is right next door to the Tax Office, so finding the mindless zombies something useful to do wasn't difficult.

You can't revitalise a dead deer by plugging it into the mains, but you can get yourself about twenty pounds of delicious flash fried venison.

If you knew Susie like I knew Susie you'd be wearing three condoms and a hazard protection suit.

In tests, 100% of squirrels fired from a cannon failed to land in one piece.

You can't teach an old dog new tricks, but you can teach it to play backgammon - a pleasant way for your canine chum to while away its' twilight years.

72% of men will overlook the fact that a woman may be a self-obsessed bore if she can suck cock like a vacuum cleaner set to stun.

Climate change is happening because no-one knows where the timer is and the heating has mysteriously set itself to 'always on'.

Toilet soap is used for cleaning the hands and face as part of one's ablutions in the bathrooms of this land. Toilet soup is a culinary anomaly invented by a pervert chef.

'I feel like chicken tonight' was a euphemism for a desire for underage sex prior to the invention of the low class chicken sauce product. The advertising agent who thought of the advert strap line was, unsurprisingly, suspected of being a paedophile.

No-one who has ever sung the 'Theme from Fame!' at a karaoke night has ever lived beyond the age of 52, despite assurances in the song to the contrary.

For reasons lost in the mists of time, the bestselling drink in the Channel Islands is liquefied Red Leicester cheese.

Popular sweet ice-cream topping "hundreds and thousands" was invented in 1907 and was originally marketed under the brand name "Shitloads".

Bob Holness did not play the sax solo in Gerry Rafferty's Baker Street contrary to the popular urban myth, but Carol Vordermann did programme the theme tune to Blockbusters and moonlights as the drum 'n' bass performer DJ Shitloans.

Sheep instinctively dig a cacophony; this is why so many of them are world renowned jazz experts.

The average speed on the Périphérique, the inner ring road of Paris, is 171mph. This compares favourably with the average speed on London's North Circular which is one mile every three days.

71% of Kwik-Fit fitters suffer from premature ejaculation.

Because as a child he'd always wanted to play the bagpipes, Dee Dee Ramone took his name from the postcode for Dundee.

The World Trade Center actually collapsed because of an infestation of metal eating ladybirds.

The Guinness Book of Records officially recognises "Quaker Boxing" as the world's most boring contact sport.

The maintenance tool of choice for really big mechanics is the gorilla wrench.

Judge Dredd was originally a 6'9" Rastafarian.

The headquarters of the United States Department of Defence is only that shape because it was designed by a really incompetent architect.

Punk rock group The Damned were all failed born-again Christians with troubled consciences.

In much the same way that people who have the surname "Fletcher" had ancestors who made arrows, and the surname "Thatcher" suggest roof-making ancestors, the ancestors of people with the name "Filmer" made low quality VHS porn movies, probably involving farm animals.

Anthracite coal is also an ore from which anthrax can be extracted as it's made from compressed prehistoric sheep.

Potato peelings and All-Bran are particularly high in moral fibre.

In the North East of England it is widely accepted that Kevin Keegan will be killed by being run over by the Shields Ferry.

The third series in the CSI franchise was due to be CSI:Midsomer, until the makers realised they couldn't come up with storylines as preposterous as those already peddled by ITV.

On his application form to join Take That, Robbie Williams listed his hobbies as "crying and being beaten up".

Dennis the Menace is an insurable hazard.

Gerry & Kate McCann run a garden supplies shop on the side specialising in pampas grass.

The most recent edition of the "Observers Book Of Things You Can Have Wrong With You" includes a chapter entitled "And here are some we made up one evening in the pub, for a laugh". Over 60% of these imaginary ailments now have internet discussion forums dedicated to sufferers and the alternative therapies used to treat them.

Were a human being to live to the age of 1000, he or she would find that their personal "odometer" would revert to zero and their life would begin again.

A traditional greeting in many parts of Hungary involves looking at someone with a bad attitude then spitting at them in the face before biting them.

If you can't spell a disease you can't contract it. This may go some way to explaining the reason why Dartford has the best health record in England.

Olives are slugs with no ambition.

MC Hammer's assertion that 'you can't touch this' was backed up by a court order.

A leaked memo from a Channel 4 board meeting has revealed a secret plan to boost ratings by adding killer bees to every programme format, starting with the evening news.

Police raids on alternative health stores in Brighton and Hove have uncovered large stocks of a hitherto unknown "natural" date-rape drug, Rosehipnol.

No-one has ever seen the business plans of the companies that make all the crap that ends up in pound shops because they don't exist. Somewhere in China is a man for whom the manufacture of knock-off Darth Vader dolls in a purple cape with a silver helmet is a vanity project.

Mothercare owns massive blocks of shares in all the worlds' manufacturers of pink dye.

In a recent television interview, ex-chairman of the Conservative Party and serial liar Jeffrey Archer revealed that "Jeffrey Archer" is merely a nom-de-plume. His given name at birth was "Jesus Christ".

Channel 4 has commissioned a Christmas Special reality show, tentatively entitled "Rub Alan Carr's Face Up And Down Against Pebble Dashing".

For three days in 1972 Mr Kipling's 'exceedingly good cakes' were made of nails, badger shit and mud, until his door was kicked in and he was carted off in a loony lorry. Manufacture of lemon slices recommenced within the hour, containing only traces of mustelidian faeces.

Drinking cyan printers ink makes your poo blue.

There is an on-going worldwide competition among advertising agencies to have the silliest name; for many years the title was held by Willoughby Willoughby Willoughby and Farting, until they were topped by a Melbourne agency called Felcher, Arsetrumpet and Spunk. All three directors were 'wacky' media students with no qualms about using Deed Polls foolishly.

Tofu is a by-product of the bacon industry.

Newcastle United football club employs a firm of Geordie physiotherapists called "Knee Worries".

At the inquest into the death of Princess Diana of Hearts, the jury was shown CCTV footage, allegedly of HRH Duke of Edinburgh doing a funny dance and singing "Ding Dong, the witch is dead!", while swigging from a bottle of swan blood. The video was time stamped at five minutes after news of the princess's untimely demise had broken on BBC News, but was ruled inadmissible as the camera in question was overlooking the Harrods car park, and the voice of Mohammed Fayed could be clearly heard in the background shouting "This'll stitch those German bastards up like kipper - refuse me a passport, eh???"

Just as Elvis said 'there's no room to rumba in a sports car' there's also no space to salsa in a sedan or indeed no point in pogoing in a police van, no matter how drunk you are.

The proposed series CSI: Droitwich was abandoned when the scriptwriters realised that episode one's core theme of the youth hanging round the war memorial was as exciting as it was going to get, and a drive-by shouting in episode two wasn't going to stretch to ten minutes let alone a whole episode.

Margaret Thatcher's maiden name was "Gobshite".

Most typographical errors are actually the same word as the intended English one, but in Welsh.

According to the old lyric, "I don't care what the weatherman says if the weatherman says it's raining"; one should however pay close attention if the weatherman says "Cthulhu fhtagn" because it means he (or she) is possessed by the High Priest of the Great Old Ones and death and destruction shall surely reign across the Earth.

The original last line of the Frank & Nancy Sinatra song was "and then I go and spoil it all by saying something stupid like 'Heghlu'meH QaQ jajvam'" until someone pointed out that the Klingon phrase for 'Today is a good day to die' was not really in keeping with the romantic ethos of the rest of the song, and the Star Trek obsessed lyricist who keeps cropping up in this damned book was sacked.

"Pentapeptides" is French for lard.

Google is trialling a mobile-phone only service called "Google Pubquiz", which provides search results in a skin cunningly designed to look like a website for an estate agent, used car dealer or STD clinic.

Earl Tupper, inventor of Tupperware, had a side-line in a calypso "super group" along with Emperor Rosko and Lord Sandwich.

Victorian etiquette dictated that it was only acceptable to add a slice of lemon to your gin and tonic if there wasn't a clove of garlic available.

Guacamole is made of the pureed remnants of victims of the fairground game, Whack-A-Mole.

Application forms for jobs with the secret service are printed out in Wingdings font and have to be returned by leaving them in a duck in Hyde Park.

Stanley knives were invented in 1902 by Stanley Malfeasance, a criminal from Whitechapel in East London who wanted to achieve the notoriety of Jack The Ripper but needed a weapon that could fatally injure whores and yet have its' blade changed in mere seconds for maximum efficiency in the challenging arena of prostitute slaughter.

The connections between computers to allow them to communicate with each other, and thus to form the "internet" were originally made with tin cans and taut strings.

In early "Mastermind" shows, if a contestant didn't know the answer, rather than simply saying "pass", they were instructed to use the phrase; "I'm sorry Magnus, but I haven't got a bastard clue."

Up until 1978, not only did the BBC regularly erase videotapes of old programmes in order to reuse the tape, they also sent out squads of hit men to assassinate anyone who'd seen the original broadcast.

"R&B" star Usher's house fell down in 2004.

The original lyric to the Stevie Wonder hit was "I just called to say I'm really a man in a dress" but Mr Wonder deemed the world wasn't ready for a song about a blind black transvestite, and watered it down somewhat.

Pigs have naturally occurring tattoos just under the skin that mark out the best cuts, for the benefit of butchers. Once bled out, they look just like bits of fat.

Double yolked eggs are laid by chickens with two arses.

The nasty, sticky, yellow drink "advocaat" is made from the nasty, sticky, green fruit, "avocado".

Lemmy has an honorary GCSE in woodwork from Staffordshire University.

Country singer Shania Twain is actually famous punk transsexual Wayne / Jayne County in a cowboy hat.

Insects and arachnids which venture too close to "Wi-Fi" routers or mobile 'phone masts will be irradiated enough for them to, should they bite you, give you superpowers.

Frank Sinatra's parents were both goths, and named their son Corpserape. He changed it by deed poll when he was 19 to ease his way into easy listening circles, but prior to his well-known shooby-dooby career, young Corpserape was the first white rap/metal crossover act in Brooklyn, in 1932.

It is customary to achieve good luck by shaking the hand of a chimney sweep. If, however, said chimney sweep is on a beach holiday, the same level of luck can be achieved by letting him take a poo in your chalet toilet.

The song 'Doctor My Eyes', a tender love song made famous by the Jacksons but written by Jackson Browne, was originally titled 'Doctor My Arse' and was about a rectal prolapse following an extended bout of unlubed anal sex.

The Star Wars character Mace Windu was named in honour of Mrs George Lucas and her over the top reaction involving a rape deterrent spray against a man who farted noisily next to her.

The singular of "bogies" is "bogus".

It's generally accepted that the most useful reference book to own when installing Microsoft Windows Small Business Server is a copy of "Tarka The Otter".

If you realise that someone you're talking to is short-sighted, it's polite to refer to their condition as "youropia".

Given that beer increases telepathic powers, it has been calculated that a man who is still conscious after drinking 24 pints of ale would have sufficient mental power to summon up a black hole and render the Hadron Collider entirely pointless. Willing victims haven't made it to pint 19 yet without passing out, at which point said telepathic powers seem to ooze out of the volunteer's mouth, disguised as dribble.

The secret invention of time travel by students at MIT have ensured that yes, Dickens and Shakespeare *are* writing soap operas these days, while JRR Tolkien is writing dramas to be shown on ITV at 8.00pm, continuing his life's work of boring the population rigid and annoying the manufacturers of sleeping remedies.

The most popular website among the youth of South Africa is an antelope-spotting website called "Facebok".

Every track on Tony Christie's album "Made In Sheffield", celebrating the songs and sounds of that fine city has a backing track of Jarvis Cocker playing the spoons.

'Help The Aged' is a Government department They round up all the old ladies - the men are all dead already - with no dependants, and execute them to save pensions money and free up housing stock. Originally titled 'Help The Aged Die and Free Themselves From Their Geriatric Housebound Misery', their name was changed to make it more palatable and less interesting to anyone who might kick up a fuss.

In cockney fiscal terms, a monkey is £500, a pony is £25 and a squirrel is £36; more recent additions to the canon are a beagle, being £17, a llama, which is £33, and an ocelot, which is £56.50.

'The Diary of Horace Wimp' by ELO was originally titled 'A Day In The Life Of Horace Wimp' but Jeff Lynne thought that was taking the piss a touch too much.

Extra lining for shoes that goes inside the shoe is an insole. A similar device that is fastened to the underside of the shoe is called an arsehole. They've never been successfully marketed because of the obvious confusion in naming and definition.

Ava Gardner's original stage name was Ava Banana, but she changed it when the old tyme music hall song was a big hit. Originally chosen to reflect her love of soft fruit, 'Ava Gardner', her second choice of pseudonym, was chosen to reflect her keen interest in sexually assaulting the domestic help.

The quickest way to charge up a laptop battery is to pop the whole laptop into the microwave on full power for about fifteen minutes.

The most popular blues band in Ireland is a tribute act by the name of "Carsick Mick".

Clive Dunn is in hiding in Spain from the hit squad which has been knocking off members of the Dad's Army cast since the show finished its original run. He wears a Salman Rushdie mask when he goes out, as he's less afraid of Iranian militants than he is of the Greg Dyke-led death squad.

In their early days, Swedish pop sensations Abba were known as Abbab, as they had a third male member - an Irishman from County Kildaire called Bejesus.

Paracetamol is a cure for victims of paracide.

There's a town in Lincolnshire called Sorrow, which features a large chain restaurant on the edge of the conurbation. The Metallica song 'Harvester of Sorrow' was written after the band stopped at said restaurant for lunch, the line 'language of the mad' being a reference to the local accent.

Colouring in your face with a highlighter pen makes your blood fizz because of the radium content.

Former MPs who underwent the standard process to remove their moral compass and were subsequently deselected as a result of putting whores, cocaine, rent boys and moat cleaning on expenses, can still eke out profitable if not worthy careers in insurance claims departments where similar levels of abject bastardy are seen as positives.

Bob Marley was a huge fan of both tennis and bridge, hence the opening line to one of his most popular songs; "One love, one heart".

Peter Bonetti was nicknamed "The Cat", a moniker resented by his sister because, in direct consequence, she was known around Streatham as Marjorie "The Dog" Bonetti.

IKEA has abandoned plans to sell home assembly artificial life forms because the positronic brains they've bought en masse can only speak Swedish and Cantonese - not much use in a global robot slave market.

It is possible to convert 240v power supplies to 110v for use on American devices by putting the American (110v) plug up your arse and placing the live 240v wires in your ears.

Celebrity Big Brother is now an acknowledged 'elephant's graveyard' for past it third rate talent. No-one who's appeared on it ever has been anything more than washed up, worn out or just totally and eternally shit.

Crocodiles floss each other's teeth to keep cavities at bay. Their little arms can't reach their own.

David Cameron is an inflated balloon filled with used cooking oil and rat faeces, which has somehow become sentient. This explains a lot.

Fab ice lollies induce euphoria and flashes of genius. Cornettos bring about bouts of rank stupidity.

As a child, Michael Gove played Pob in a live action movie version of the children's TV programme.

Boris Johnson's hair is cleverer than he is.

Dementia isn't the involuntary degradation of mental faculty as is often perceived - it's just old people thinking 'fuck it they can deal with this shit now', not bothering anymore and being a colossal pain in the arse.

Jessie J was cloned from 1980s scouse songstress Sonia.

It's impossible to have any sort of satisfactory sexual relations with a pineapple.

Apple Corp. will subjugate us all by 2025 - and we'll be forced to not only enjoy it but buy the tools of our oppression.

Popular children's toy 'Bop It' originally had an additional command being 'Fuck It' whereby the player had to hurl the device at the nearest wall while swearing loudly. Curiously players have retained this option while the actual toy no longer features it.

The easiest way to remove excess body hair from legs, chest, ears or nasal passages is with a butane powered weed wand.

Scientists have invented a washing machine that can completely remove the stink from sports shoes, but they are loathe to release it to market because of the nuclear devastation it causes in the process and the subsequent threat of lawsuits.

Calippo ice lollies were developed for kids suffering from polio.

The Holy Bible has a Catholic Edition because their deeply held man made lies are slightly different to those of Protestants.

Yummy Mummies taste bloody horrible.

The modern street urchin has taken to wearing a baseball cap with a brim all the way round, rather than just at the back. This keeps the sun off the neck, out of the eyes, and prevents the tops of the ears from reddening. Among the youth this item is known as a fedora.

Red wine cures everything, including alcoholism.

Fast food is only truly fast food if it's served on a Eurostar as it travels through France. Otherwise it's correctly referred to as 'lukewarm grey shit in a stale bun'.

The last Famous Five book (which was never published) covered their blossoming sexuality, the discovery of home grown cannabis, and their near fatal attempts by Julian and Dick to mimic the Jackass series of stunt programmes while stoned off their gourds in order to impress the members of their gang of the opposite sex.

The effect of listening to Coldplay was the inspiration for the Zalgo series of images, featuring lost souls, bleeding eyes, and hideous monstrosity type mutations.

A Kindle can store up to 1400 books, or more than thirty thousand if they all squeeze up a bit.

The sister ship of HMS Conqueror, the nuclear submarine, was HMS Fighting-After-Eight-Pints-Of-Stella, which was a Dover-Calais ferry.

Yohei Taniike is a Japanese football player as well as a Samurai battle cry.

The Wikipedia entry for 'telecommunications in Latvia' reads 'Nope.'

Classic cars with big wings, if placed rear end first on the ground, look like silhouettes of ladies with massive bosoms.

There is a disused branch of the Victoria Line on the London Underground that runs all the way to Great Yarmouth. It was built at the behest of Churchill who found the waters there soothed his haemorrhoids.

"May I interest yourself in our great deals this week?"

Telesales people are frequently recruited from the undead. They figure that if their souls are in torment, yours should be too.

Pedro Almodóvar's first full length movie was a documentary about tunnel boring techniques in the Pyrenees, and not the overtly sexual movies his Wiki page claims.

Glenfield Hospital, just outside Leicester, is the world's number one centre for Investigating Why People Shove Weird Stuff Up Their Own Arses.

Catalan public sports TV channel Esport3 shows a football programme entitled "FutbolCat" which is presented by a trio of felines. Only one is awake at any one time, though all three will startle and flee should a goal be scored. The programme features long pauses while the cats are coaxed out of the rafters to allow the programme to continue.

Wiener Sport-Club, a football club from Vienna in Austria, has an eight foot tall flaccid penis as its mascot.

The Runyang Bridge crosses the Yangtze River in China. It links Zhenjiang on the south bank of the river and, by means of a wormhole, the planet Kepler-16, 196 light years from Earth. Traffic only flows one way.

Teignmouth has a constant smell of unwashed vagina because of the huge whore farms on the outskirts of town. Although closed in 1978, the all-pervading stench remains. The farms were converted into luxury flats but are only appealing to those persons with no sense of smell.

The first English football league was made up of three teams who played each other in rotation every weekend for 39 weeks at the behest of FIFA. They were Preston North End, Arsenal, and Wisbech Academicals, who went out of business in 1902.

"The Woman in Me (Needs the Man in You)" is a song by Shania Twain about trans-sexual anal violation. You work it out.

The holy order Sisters of the Holy Infant Jesus is blasphemous in suggesting that Mary had a multitude of female children after giving birth to Christ. She had two more boys, called Roger and William.

In the TV show Fawlty Towers, Sybil Fawlty's hair contained a live marmoset.

Celebrity Big Brother is under investigation from the Advertising Standards Authority since no-one has a bastard clue who these no-marks cluttering up our tellies are.

In the US the National Commission On The Average Size Of Feet, Penis And Hat was only disbanded in 1995, 21 years after its last report. No-one knows why it was founded in the first place, although it's known that Nixon was somewhat obsessed with the topic and no-one on his staff had feet over size 6 (US sizing), nor a penis longer than four and a half inches. One notable choad, belonging to an intern in the FBI, was five and one eighth inches in diameter. It's thought Nixon found this hilarious and let the unfortunate individual stay on.

The digital divide is a global phenomenon, separating those with high speed internet access and those still reliant on Ceefax. Ceefax was killed off for the masses in early 2012 yet persists due to local enthusiasts updating the pages with articles regarding local news, weather, and jumble sales.

Most praying mantises are agnostic.

The University Of Life is based in Droitwich. It has outposts in Des Moines, Krakow, and Perth.

Ice hockey was invented by psychotic fishmongers armed with cleavers. The handles of these weapons were lengthened to allow the easy chopping of conger eels.

American Indian 'peace pipes' usually contain Old Holborn.

American men named Randy are often infertile, and are frequently over-compensating.

Argentinian Golf is a variant on the game in which random holes contain a potentially deadly charge of C4, just to liven an otherwise dreary game up a bit. Holes in one are obviously free of risk to the player but a putt from six inches may be fatal.

Sweden is crammed with fjords because God was suffering from Parkinson's Disease when he planned it out.

Sea snails can hold their breath for up to four years.

Dar Es Salaam is the default destination for drunks in taxis.

Coolderry, a small roadside village in southern County Offaly, Ireland, is the least trendy place in Europe - even less so than Belgium.

The Stamford Museum and Nature Center, located in Stamford, Connecticut, contains a collection of marital aids as used by the first thirty-two American Presidents. The tradition of passing these through the line ended when Harry S. Truman became the 33rd President and declared that "I shall not partake of anal beads used by Calvin Coolidge nor Herbert Hoover, let alone by both of those fine upstanding and yet excessively sexually adventurous gentlemen." He was also doubtful of Martin Van Buren's cock ring.

The New York Cosmos training facility is on Mars.

The snakes known as vipers kill their prey by injecting them with warfarin through their fangs. They have been successfully domesticated and used to control rat populations.

Cranoglanis is the Latin name of the genus of armorhead catfishes, but translates literally as 'dickhead'.

Blooming Valley, Pennsylvania was originally Fucking Bastard Gorge but the cartographer realised next day that making up names whilst drunk and furious with one's own shortcomings wasn't the wisest of moves.

In 1821 in Denmark, absolutely nothing happened at all.

Toowong is a suburb of Brisbane, Australia and is named after its founder who had a bifurcated penis.

Certain orchids can be arranged such that when sliced through and eaten together they taste like trifle. It's a lot cheaper to buy a real trifle.

Street maps for London and Tripoli are identical, except that the Libyan city map is in Arabic. The insurrection of 2011 against

Colonel Gadaffi was centred around the equivalent of Parson's Green.

The first velodrome at Aldersley was built in 1752, some ninety years before the bicycle was invented. It was originally used for wheelbarrow racing, with the possibility of go-karting every Sunday.

American rapper Dr Dre bought his doctorate from the same place as Gillian McKeith.

The Heatherslaw Light Railway in Northumberland runs for a total length of 35 metres between stations. It's quicker to get out and walk than wait for the tender to get up to steam. Because it follows standard ticketing price structures, a single adult ticket costs £9.30. A return is 20 pence more.

The Star Spangled Banner was written by Abul A'la Maududi, an Islamic fundamentalist, and the original star referred to was that of the Pakistani national flag.

Clare Torry is a British singer who famously performed the wordless vocals on Pink Floyd's "The Great Gig in the Sky" on the 1973 album The Dark Side of the Moon. She suffers intense claustrophobia and could not bear to be standing in any sort of canyon, preferring the plains of deepest Wiltshire.

John Terry has been classified as vermin in thirteen UK counties and can be shot on sight.

Will.i.am is an elaborate practical joke.

Scientists are attempting to determine if Carlos Tevez is a new genus of ape.

Future series of the smash hit BBC genealogy programme "Who Do You Think You Are?" will be named "Who The Fuck Are You Anyway?" after complaints from non-K-list-celebrity-obsessed viewers.

Prime Minister David Cameron was recently hauled in front of the Parliamentary Expenses Committee after claiming over a thousand pounds against his monthly purchases of Pledge in order to maintain his hideous shiny face.

Not only did Florence Nightingale invent a very specific form of pie chart, she also came up with the casserole diagram, the risotto graph and the three dimensional pizza schematic.

While many US States have laws allowing idiots to opt-out of vaccinations for their children on religious grounds, the same laws also allow right thinking people to take the self-same morons and refuseniks and burn them at the stake with no fear of prosecution on grounds of public sanitation.

David Bellamy is genetically 50% rhododendron bush.

The Inuit edition of Wikipedia lists 931 different words for snow.

Authors cannot claim moral rights for works of pornography.

At the BAFTA awards in 2006, every single award went to the children's TV show 'Tikkabilla' in one way or another.

The TAF15 gene only occurs in Welsh people, hence the name.

William Coupon was a photographer who documented the New York punk scene but his family fortune was based on the invention of money off vouchers for use in supermarkets.

Ted Nugent's grandfather was named Ted Oldgent in his later years.

The national anthem of Paraguay is the Lambeth Walk.

Sunni Muslims are noted for their cheery dispositions.

Joe Pasquale is not a castrato, and has fathered fourteen children all of whom are basso profundo, even the girls.

TV show 'Most Haunted' was due to record a special from Jackie Onassis' vagina before she herself died.

Social networking tool Twitter is actually simply a random number generator plugged into a dictionary.

Twitter was so named because "bleatingfuckers.com" was already taken.

Use of social networking tool "LinkedIn" involves agreeing to terms and conditions which sell your soul to Satan and promise you an eternity of torment and hellfire in return for some vaguely relevant job adverts every now and again.

Nick Clegg is a fictional entity based on the showroom dummies in the Doctor Who episode "Terror of the Autons".

Garden rotavators, available at quite reasonable prices from DIY superstores make ideal stress-busting massagers for highly strung or unruly cats. They're pretty much guaranteed not to wee on your duvet again.

The original reason for building microphones into laptop computers was to give Microsoft Visual Studio the ability to send a developer's pleading cry of "Please – just fucking work!" direct to Bill Gates' office. He collects them on CD and listens to them as an alternative to whale song on nights when he can't get to sleep.

The winning team on University Challenge 1982 was from the University of Life.

Writing "Jedi" in the religion box on the national census really is the cleverest thing ever. It's been proven.

Small animal supermarket "Pets At Home" was initially named "Pet Cemetery" as all the animals they sell are evil tempered bastards who appear to have returned from the grave.

Shi'ite Muslims are considered by other followers of the Islamic faith to be a bit rubbish.

A poll in 1997 of favourite sandwich fillings revealed that by far the most satisfying option was minced solicitor.

Photocopiers render any testicle placed on the glass infertile, thankfully.

The World Trade Center was the global hub for the duplication of Betamax tapes. Of the 2606 people that died in the attacks, only 3 were professional tape loaders as there wasn't much demand by then.

Cricketer Andrew Strauss' dad was named Levi and invented denim trousers.

New Orleans keeps getting hit by hurricanes because God hates jazz and blues, preferring hip hop and speed metal.

American politician and halfwit Mitt Romney was named after his mother's favourite item of winter clothing. She too was distinctly 'special'.

There are several dozen unexploded bombs from World War Two scattered across Europe, which are expected to spontaneously explode due to corrosion and subsequent failure of safety devices, within the next twenty years or so. The damage caused is expected to be in excess of forty billion Euros, with a loss of more than thirty thousand lives. Official Government advice is to move to Swindon, the town that's officially considered "too boring to contain bombs", but this is creating a surge in property prices such that a three bed semi in Covingham, an unremarkable suburb to the north east of Swindon, has risen from £160,000 in 2011 to in excess of three quarters of a million pounds.

Black Daleks celebrate Kwanzaa, gold ones Passover, and grey ones nothing at all because they're Methodists.

Permaculture is the process of introducing chemically induced hairstyles to places like Perth in Western Australia.

One can return cars with whining gearboxes back to the manufacturer for rectification; the option to do the same with whining children was withdrawn in 1981 by Thatcher's Tory government.

A lemon sorbet has been created in Sardinia that is sufficiently sour tactually turn one's head inside out.

Most sentient fire alarms are actually quite languid about the whole conflagration thing, accepting that it is their fate to die in a smouldering puddle of charred plastic.

Previously "thrash" and now "tedious" metal band Metallica have several insurance claims against them outstanding since the mid-1980s, mainly for whiplash injuries.

"Intelligent design" was originally an April Fool's joke from the 1920s that got way out of hand when religious fundamentalists from Kansas heard about it.

The "Mars Rover", successfully landed on the Red Planet by NASA in a remarkable feat of aeronautics and engineering is actually built on the chassis of a Morris Marina and not a Rover at all, although both motor manufacturers fell under the aegis of British Leyland.

Mitt Romney's nickname among his close friends and business associates is 'Oven Glove'.

Most shower gels are flavoured with lemon, lime, tea tree oil, coconut and similar. This is because a retail experiment using goat flavoured shower gel failed dismally at the audience acceptance stage, and no-one's been brave enough to render any sort of carcass for bodily cleanliness since.

The most effective diet plan in the world involves stapling one's lips and nostrils together, making the ingress of any food impossible. Unfortunately it also makes breathing problematic without a tracheotomy, a fundamental flaw in an otherwise immaculate plan.

Justin Bieber is a little girl with a strap on secreted in her jeans.

The New Seekers were formed in the early 70s, using their family friendly band image as a cover for an investigative unit much like Scooby Doo and the Mystery Gang, spending eight years trying to find the original Seekers who had gone off seeking and never reported back.

Formal Theory is an axiomatic system, something representable by symbols and its operators. It's also the theory that it's much easier to get laid while wearing a dinner jacket.

Every member of Australian rock band The Living End was formally declared dead at some point before they recorded their first album.

Sarah Jessica Parker looks like that because of some plastic surgery she had performed as a teen which involved material literally taken from a horse's arse.

Basildon was built using slave labour, which explains the general quality issues.

The Scottish Fold is a breed of cat with inbuilt hinges.

The Silk Road stretched from China across to Italy and was a major trading route for centuries, but always avoided going overland to the North and hence through Austria because oompah music makes silk turn to nylon.

Palestinian freedom of movement is a specific series of yoga disciplines, designed to loosen muscles in the back and free up the West Bank.

Dutch death metal band Prostitute Disfigurement are best known for penning the 'Mmm Danone' TV advert.

Philosophers can be effectively turbocharged by adding lager.

Everyone from Rotherham is either a Satanist, a Methodist or a cyclist.

Popular traditional English brewery 'Marstons' has recently launched a new brand of "Surreal Ale" which tastes of fish and melting clocks.

Popular beat combo 'The Moody Blues' were originally known as the Ratty Bastards.

Buckingham Palace was originally a tent before the extensions were added. The original canvas core rotted away in the 1980s.

You can only have a career in marketing if your soul is made of brimstone. Real people are naturally repulsed by it.

Peppermint tea is made with the hides of recently deceased corgis and not peppers, mints, or any variance thereof.

Ribaldry, being the art of near the knuckle saucy humour, was originally 'taking the piss out of blokes with comb overs'.

FIFA's Bribes Division has more employees and a higher financial turnover than the population and GDP of Belgium.

Canada's flag features a maple leaf because the original artist couldn't draw hands.

Scientists are working on a football kit so garish that it will stun referees and allow astonishing levels of cheating including handball, murder, and having a team of 27 players on the pitch simultaneously.

The word 'cunt' has never appeared in the lyric of a country and western song.

If bananas are allowed to turn brown, they will taste of dog poo.

80% of email never arrives because it has to pass through older firewalls where emails are treated like witches - if it burns, it's innocent; if it doesn't, it's offering you a larger penis. These firewalls are kept in heavily insulated server rooms which resemble hell, what with the fire, smoke, ashes and such. Your local sysadmin makes a credible Satan alternative.

Dipsomania is so named because of sufferers' tendency to stagger, weave and fall down.

The law isn't so much an ass as a demented baboon, slinging shit at all and sundry.

Darwinism is slowly being outlawed to protect those who would normally be too stupid to live.

Janet Jackson's abandoned prog rock album was entitled 'Too Fat To Live, Too Stupid To Die' and was based on the life and times of Bernard Manning.

Whale semen is fluorescent orange and is often mistaken for particularly attractive jellyfish. Both will result in conjunctivitis if you get it in your eyes.

The most extreme Paralympic category is for competitors with no limbs, no head, and no torso. No-one has ever entered this category and yet there are forty two gold medals up for grabs every four years.

Sheridan Smith is banned from most churches and cathedrals in the UK for fear that if she were to laugh several priceless stained glass windows would shatter.

Prince Charles' testicles are actually two walnuts in one of his mum's old pairs of tights, tied around his Little Man.

Rapper Jay-Z suffers from dysentery of the mouth.

Rod Hull's Emu was a keen enthusiast of the genteel art of fisting.

The staff at the Simon Weisenthal Center secretly hope the Nazis developed some sort of longevity drug 70 years ago, or else they'll be rendered obsolete soon.

The sequel to We Need To Talk About Kevin is called No-One's Overly Concerned About Ashleigh Because She's Very Normal And Pretty And A Bit Dull, But Loves Her Cat. It's not sold quite swell, given the main plot device is a scratching fight in the playground after someone said Mr Tibbles was a 'fat old fleabag', rather than a high school massacre.

Billy Ray Cyrus' Achey Breaky Heart has now completely crumbled away, having been eaten by rodents and moths.

A lager powered belch, if correctly focussed, is louder than a backfiring motorcycle.

The bassoon was invented as a method of disguising rampant flatulence.

Any man of more than eight feet in height can expect to suffer taxidermy after his death, and to be turned into some sort of coat rack with his outstretched hands utilised as grotesque hooks.

Tasmanian devils are only that irritable because of their appalling haemorrhoids.

The town of Nutbush has replaced the church-house and the gin-house at the city limits with a strip mall and a selection of chain fast food restaurants.

In the 2011 Iranian General Election, 112% of the population voted for Mahmoud Ahmadinejad - many people voting more than once in a display of patriotic fervour.

Hugo Chávez, President of Venezuela, invented the Burberry check.

The Boston Strangler came from Lincolnshire.

Eating five portions a day of fruit and/or vegetables will significantly improve your health. Eating ten a day will make you a genius within three months, fifteen portions will make you a Superman by the end of the year, and twenty a day will give you the galloping shits.

The meerkats from the comparethemarket.com all contracted rabies in 2012, and that's why the characters appearing on screen today are puppets - they're made from the taxidermied corpses of the original cast who were inhumanely put down in the manner of unwanted kittens, using a sack, a rope, some bricks and a handy canal. The rope was tied around the sack and used to drag it back out after a day or so.

Jimi Hendrix was a virgin until he became famous - his song "Are You Experienced" was a coded message to ladies to teach him what goes where.

Turf especially grown for use in urban gardens has three types of grass for hardy growth and fox shit spores pre-sown. If correctly nurtured this can flourish into a full adult sized fox log, three per square meter. This will help attract urban foxes to your back garden so you can be serenaded at night by the sweet and delicate sound of their sensuous lovemaking.

The 'all-nighter' movie sessions at the Scala in London famously showed nothing between 2 and 5am because everyone was asleep.

Electric toothbrushes, when correctly applied, can supercharge your brain by feeding a stream of positive ions.

David Blaine features in the Guinness Book Of Records as "World's Least Popular Children's Party Magician".

Dog excrement is popular as foundation make-up in certain parts of Essex.

While many rock bands took their name from the book and film "A Clockwork Orange" (Heaven 17, Moloko etc.), both Napalm Death and Slayer got their monikers from an episode of Bagpuss.

Scientists have managed to make a Friday afternoon last seventeen hours.

Michael Jackson wrote to Jimmy Savile when he was a kid. The rest is history.

There is an on-going debate as to whether women with moustaches should wax to depilate or wax to groom, eventually growing a beautiful and imposing handlebar.

The unsettling and odd goings-on in the village of Royston Vasey in 'The League Of Gentlemen' is based upon the writers' childhood experiences in Lincoln whilst visiting spinster aunts.

The original recipe for the Heston Blumenthal Christmas Pudding had the hidden orange replaced by a dog egg from an Irish Wolfhound.

Shane McGowan is what Alastair McGowan looks like when he's not impersonating anyone.

Genghis and Chaka were first cousins.

High level skydiver Felix Baumgartner changed his name from Frank Bumgardener.

Writing irate letters to The Times in green pen makes you appear to be an intellectual, even if you're actually semi simian.

Princesses should be aware that while there's only a very small chance that a kissed frog may turn into a handsome prince, there are odds of about one in three that it will turn into a man eating tiger and bite your head off.

Tom and Jerry were lovers off screen and taught Richard Gere everything he knows.

One in three civil servants pushes papers and achieves nothing.

The world is actually ruled by a shadowy cabal called the Buildabear Group.

Terry Wogan's natural accent is a broad Norfolk one, and his jocular Irish radio persona is only there to calm the frightened and confused who make up his listener base.

Sexual harassment in the workplace cases increase eight-fold in the last two months of the year as a combined result of drunken Christmas parties and the increasing popularity of Movember and the resultant sex-pest look which men will naturally strive to meet in all aspects. Early Christmas parties in late November are especially fraught, averaging 8.2 unlikely, regrettable though enthusiastic bouts of sexual congress, often in the bogs or on the Chairman's desk.

The Ace of Spades is outranked in every card game by Mr Bun the Baker.

Tea is halal but not kosher. This differentiation is thought to be more political than religious.

Pop group One Direction can only move forward and have roller bearings in their shoes to allow successful negotiation around small obstacles with the help of their assistants.

The One Direction promotional crisps have been indefinitely shelved because the Harry Styles tribute ones tasted like mouldy cardboard. Nonetheless, consumer research has shown them to be of significantly higher quality than any of the 'music' the corporate ninnies are alleged to produce.

EDL members can be identified by special markings on their giros. The marking says 'twat' and is obfuscated in the serial number of their signing on books.

Jack Whitehall's natural accent is Brooklyn, NY.

Polyesters are gaudily coloured rodents, about the size of a guinea-pig, which are highly prized for their fur. Originally native to China, they're now found all over most of east Asia, and are hunted with bow and arrow by teams of highly trained orphan hunters.

The most popular pub snack in Essex is a type of soggy potato slice, boiled in beer, and sold under the brand name "Flaps".

The chances of a 'home vasectomy' actually working when the instruments used are a standard office stapler and a mildly blunt kitchen knife are only one in twelve. That's a lot of pain for a good chance of no gain.

Highlighter pens, when used to colour in your own eyeballs, will allow you to see in the dark. Yellow works best.

Tea served in a mug with a heavy metal band logo on the side will stay hot for up to fourteen hours. This is because of the innate quivering power and metal glory that exists within the earthenware item maintaining a fine but viable vibrating field that exudes heat.

Elmo from Sesame Street used his earnings to put himself through college and not only has an MBA this name but a chain of dog grooming salons. He has never achieved a fully tumescent erection.

Justin Bieber is entirely flammable if doused in petrol prior to applying a match.

Man's derision at his fellow man increases exponentially as he gets older. What is a mere triviality at the age of 21 will induce an apoplectic rage twenty years later. This is why self-entitled opinionated idiots die early - heart attacks, strokes, and assassinations by more level headed members of society who are sick of their shit.

If honeycomb is exposed to air for more than a couple of hours it reverts back to its natural state of being bees. This is why Crunchies are chocolate coated.

Hugh Fernley-Whittingstall's real surname contains three letters that do not exist in any human alphabet in this dimension, and are only audible to dogs.

By the year 2035, the average mobile phone will be three feet wide and weigh a half hundredweight. It shall be transported in a custom made suitcase on wheels. On the upside, it will contain a camera, a toaster oven, a laptop computer, a complete home medical check kit and a set of tarot cards. The kitchen sink will however be virtual.

Popular in the 80s indie/grebo band Gaye Bykers On Acid were actually abstemious, celibate, and none of them were licensed to operate any machinery, neither automobile or motorcycle. The drummer (Kev) did once have a go on a forklift.

EU mandates state that every workplace must contain at least two utter dickheads who are there to try and 'fuck up your day'. Preference for these roles are given to oily dickwads with classic bald/beard combos who were probably bullied mercilessly at school and rightly so.

Office politics is a martial art practiced by those not getting any marital action.

Mushrooms have gills so they can breathe in gravy.

Most people are promoted because of their skills in kissing arse, not in their actual jobs.

The Abba song "Does Your Mother Know" is about the revelation of one's homosexuality tone's parents, hence the repeated refrain of 'does your mother know that you're out?'

James May's hair is actually the 14th Duke of Carlisle, on a sabbatical.

The mere smell of cat faeces has better adhesive properties than actual human faeces to a blanket. Washing may not remove the smell and often the only solution is to burn it.

The average member of the UK Independence Party would like to see the return of slavery, the death penalty and the declaration of war against the rest of the world by the Glorious British Nation. The rest of the UK would like to see the entirety of UKIP shat into space, the xenophobic bastards.

Candidates for degrees in Business Studies are required to show their certificates proving their ethics and humanity have been removed alongside their A level and swimming certificates.

87% of quasi-Governmental organizations are a complete waste of time and money.

Three hundred and sixty degree reviews in the workplace have shown that most employees believe their managers to be sorely lacking in Suicide Skills, and consider they should receive practical training as soon as possible.

People with average names are average.

The practise of disowning family members because they're "utter bastards" has increased four-fold in the last ten years.

It is considered lucky to name a pet cat after a disliked sibling's child.

No-one in advertising or marketing is smart enough to understand why a cheese with the brand name Fetid failed.

Scientists are working on a collapsible bicycle that actually is small enough to shove up your arse.

An Index
Of Lies

or

An Index of
Penguin Gynaecology
(~~Third~~ Seventy-ninth Edition)

257

258

261

264

267

270

274

276

277

279

281

About The Authors

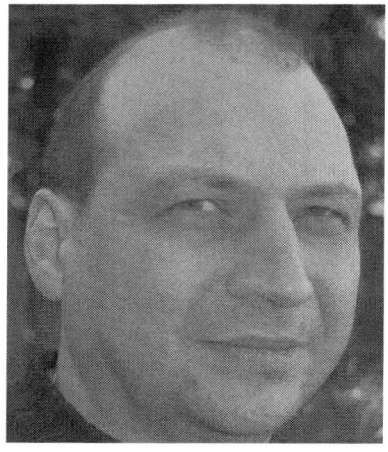

Richard Lockwood is a renowned space adventurer, psychic detective, time traveller and gentleman who spends the rest of his time developing websites. His hobbies include fending off bankruptcy and being tired.

Steve Potz-Rayner lives in Hampshire with his wife and son and tries not to break anything. He is noted for his enthusiasm of anything that involves petrol, amplifiers or beer, and ideally all three at the same time. His favourite foods are beer, bacon and fried egg rolls, and alphabet sweets and his motto is unpalatable at best and illegal in many countries even between consenting adults.

About The Illustrator

Angela Creasey lives in Lancashire with her son and her cat and wonders how she ever got mixed up with these people. Then she remembers and shudders.

NOTES

NOTES

NOTES

HEADS SHOULDERS KNEES AND TOES

KNEES AND TOES

30500140R00177

Made in the USA
Charleston, SC
18 June 2014